Rescued from Obscurity 2

... the continuing story of the ...
Hereford and Gloucester Canal - Edition 2

"Throughout the length and breadth of England, no major navigation is so lost in obscurity as the Hereford and Gloucester Canal"

David Bick, in his introduction to "The Hereford and Gloucester Canal", written in 1979. By kind permission of the Oakwood Press

Herefordshire and Gloucestershire Canal Trust

Working *together* in the present to revive the past and secure a better future.©

Rebuilding 34 miles of canal between Gloucester and Hereford

Registered Charity No. 1010721

Rescued from Obscurity

First published in Great Britain in 2014 by The Herefordshire and Gloucestershire Canal Trust.

Second Edition published 2023.

Copyright © Richard Skeet.

Richard Skeet has asserted his moral right to be identified as the author of this work.

The right of Richard Skeet to be identified as the author of this work has been asserted in accordance with Section 77 of the Copyright, Designs and Patents Act, 1988.

All rights reserved. This book is sold subject to the condition that it shall not, by way of trade or otherwise, be lent, resold, hired out, or otherwise circulated without the publisher's prior consent in any form of binding or cover other than that in which it is published and without a similar condition including this condition being imposed on the subsequent publisher.

British Library Cataloguing Data

A catalogue record for this book is available from the British Library

ISBN 978-0-9929441-1-7

Designed by Nick Dymott

Unless specifically stated, opinions expressed are those of the author and do not necessarily reflect the policy of the Herefordshire and Gloucestershire Cabal Trust.

Printed by Print Plus, 126, Widemarsh Street, Hereford, HR4 9HN

The Herefordshire and Gloucestershire Canal Trust is a non-profit distributing company limited by guarantee (No. 2704407), and is registered as a Charity (No. 1010721).

Cover photo:
Heritage boats lie at rest in the restored Over Basin *(Debbie Barber)*

Title page photo:
Skew Bridge at Monkhide *(H&GCT digital archive)*

Rescued from Obscurity

Contents

Acknowledgements	i
Foreword	iii
Introduction	1
Hereford and the River Wye	4
Early Schemes	8
Gloucester to Ledbury	16
Ledbury to Hereford	32
A Remarkable Man	41
Uncertain Times	51
Accidents and Crimes	67
Dark Ages	78
A New Beginning	92
The Herefordshire and Gloucestershire Canal Trust	102
Restoration in Herefordshire	112
Restoration in Gloucestershire	130
Llanthony Lock	165
Commercial and Environmental Sustainability	170
The Canal Trust's Fleet	179
The Canal in the Community	183
Other Reminders	188
The Road Ahead	196
Appendix	204
Index	207
Canal Walks	209
Get involved …	211

Acknowledgements

I find it difficult to imagine how this book could have been written without the help and support from members of the Hereford and Gloucester Canal Trust and others who have supplied me with advice, information, photographs, source material and practical help both for this and the first edition.

Sadly, several have passed away since 2014, but I still record my thanks.

I am particularly grateful to Glen Atkinson, Ted Beagles, David Blagrove, Roger Byard, John Chappell, Peter Cross-Rudkin, Graham Every, Colin Dymott, Brian Fox, Chris High, Pamela Hurle, Nigel Jefferies, Caroline Jones, Maggie Jones, Michael Hanford, Paul Henshaw, Chris Johnson, Wilf Jones, Alan McBride, Peter Moore, Janet Moult, Cliff Penny, David Penny, Dr. Sylvia Pinches, Mike Potts, Neil Smith, Robin Stiles, and Martyn Tilford, who between them supplied most of the photographs, archive material and advice. Sadly, constraints of space meant that I was not able to use everything I was given that I would have wished to.

I am grateful to other individuals who provided photographs and these are credited in the text wherever possible. In some cases the owner of the photograph may not have been the original photographer. Great care has been taken to ensure that illustrations have been accurately credited but that has not always been achievable and, particularly in the case of older photographs, it is possible that mistakes have been made. The author apologises for this and welcomes any corrections which are necessary.

Particular thanks are due to Lyn Ballard for kindly allowing me to quote heavily from Stephen Ballard's diaries and to reproduce his portrait. I am grateful also to Dr. Mark Baldwin for permission to quote from Charles Hadfield's letter to David Bick and to James Hervey-Bathurst for providing the Foreword. Richard Cornwell, Lauren Price (Hereford Library), John Hammond and Dr. David Skeet all provided valuable practical help.

Photographs of the Canal Company's Minute Books taken by the author are reproduced by permission of the Canal and River Trust and the National Archives, Kew.

Every effort has been made to ensure that no copyright or personal material has been used without permission. Again, should any mistakes have been made, the author apologises and welcomes any necessary corrections.

Rescued from Obscurity

I am grateful to the following for their permission to use published or archived material:

British Newspaper Archive	Ledbury Reporter
Hereford Journal	Logaston Press
Hereford Library	The Canal and River Trust
Hereford Archive Service	The National Archives
Hereford Times	Waterways World
Ledbury Civic Society	Worcester News

I am grateful to Janet Moult for her encouragement, especially when things weren't going well, and also to Debbie Barber and Gillian Northcott Liles for proofreading this edition.

Almost the last word of thanks must go to Nick Dymott who, without complaining, converted my amateur attempts at laying out this book into something which now looks like something worth reading.

Finally though, I must thank Pat, my wife, who, once again, has given me constant support, and excused me from many of the household chores, but above all, has kept me sane. Almost.

Dick Skeet

June 2023

Foreword

I am delighted that Dick Skeet has revised and updated David Bick's "***The Hereford & Gloucester Canal***" which I enjoyed reading when it first came out. He has done a very good job.

As a boy, I had explored the tunnels at Oxenhall and Ashperton and also travelled to Gloucester and back on the branch line, but without appreciating its intimate connection with the canal, and so the original book provided a great source of interesting local information on those important transport links. My family's links to the canal are obvious, not only through my mother's ancestor, Earl Somers, but also because all the external building stone for Eastnor Castle was transported from the quarries in the Forest of Dean by canal to Ledbury so, without the canal, I am sure construction of the house would have been much slower and more expensive. I am very much aware of the importance of the canal in our own family history.

This publication comes at a time when the restoration of the canal is well under way in various sectors through the hard-working volunteers in the Herefordshire & Gloucestershire Canal Trust; it is well timed and will lend weight to the efforts to finish the project, which will be a very valuable asset for local tourism and for wildlife. I hope it will also encourage wider support for the project from members of the public and grant-giving bodies.

I look forward to a delivery of new Forest of Dean sandstone by canal in due course, made possible partly as a result of this excellent revised history.

James Hervey-Bathurst CBE DL
Eastnor Castle, Ledbury
Vice President - Herefordshire & Gloucestershire Canal Trust

Introduction

... to the second edition.
Late in 2022 the Canal Trust realised that it had run out of copies of the first edition of Rescued From Obscurity but there was still a demand for it. Rather than a reprint, the Trust Board decided that now was the time to produce a second edition, "Oh, and by the way, to be ready for the start of the 2023 event season".

For the first edition I had had the great benefit of Maggie Jones' professional skills to salvage something from my rough attempts at the design of the book and I am extremely grateful for Nick Dymott, who is now doing the technical production for The Wharfinger, for taking on this role.

While much of the text has not changed a great deal, especially that dealing with past events, the opportunity has been taken to correct some mistakes and to update on what has happened since 2014. In order to keep the book to a reasonable size some material from the first edition has been omitted, but there are two new chapters which I felt were important, one relating to commercial and ecological sustainability and the other about the use of the canal by community groups.

While there was reference to these matters in the first edition, they have since become even more important, particularly in these post-Brexit, post-pandemic times, when European money will no longer be available and the public have found a new appreciation of water, green spaces and the open air.

Introduction to the first edition.
When I foolishly agreed to update the late David Bick's book, "The Hereford and Gloucester Canal" which was first published in 1979 and ran to a third edition in 2003, I envisioned a slimmer, less academic volume with a smaller amount about the past and more about the present and the future.

I intended to tell the story of the canal, as far as possible, in the words of the people of the time using newspaper cuttings, letters, Parliamentary Proceedings, Company Minutes, Stephen Ballard's dairies and the like. The elegant language of Georgian and Victorian England, if now often sounding somewhat pompous and stuffy, sometimes makes us smile - but we are the better for that.

Whether or not this was a bad mistake I leave my readers to decide, but the result was a huge amount of material to be sifted and organised. Then the emails and phone calls from members of the Trust began to arrive providing me with even more bits and pieces, so fascinating, to me at least, that there was nonc I wanted

Introduction

to exclude. My hopes of brevity soon disappeared as rapidly as water is wasted from a leaky lock.

I also wanted to speak to an audience wider than industrial archaeologists and to include the sort of people we bump into at the Canal Trust's events, both local and far from the two counties – the sort of people who tell me that they have lived all their lives in Hereford but were only vaguely aware that there was once a canal in the heart of the city.

I thought it was important not to attempt to write the Fourth Edition of David Bick's book, but to try to bring something new to the story. Probably more than anything else, David's deep knowledge of the canal's history and his determination that the memory of it should not disappear altogether, was the single most important factor in the establishment of the Hereford and Gloucester Canal Society in 1983.

It is somewhat ironic that the man who 'started it all' never really believed that full restoration of the canal was a possibility. In his later years he must have felt rather like Dr. Frankenstein whose creation got so badly out of control. In this important respect David and I part company, for I believe that, if we want it enough, one day there will be boats arriving in Hereford having travelled all the way by canal from Gloucester and far beyond.

While the correct title of the canal was the "Herefordshire and Gloucestershire Canal Navigation", I have followed the convention of most authors and adopted the shorter title of "Hereford and Gloucester Canal". I think the minutes clerk recording the proceedings of the Company Committee and General Assembly would have envied me.

Since the names of some of the locks on the canal do not appear on early maps I have used the lock names as they appear in the Minute Books. Most of these will be familiar, but "Thingwell" Lock which appears in Bick's book and almost everything else since, I believe to be a corruption of "Thinghill". The Minute Books mention "Kymin" Lock which is a far more logical name.

More mysteriously we read that Humpidge's Lock and Morgan's Lock were in need of new gates in 1831, oak timber for new gates at Bullock's Lock, Newent had been purchased in 1867 and, strangest of all, that in 1840 "the Lock gates are being put in to the Skewbridge Lock." Whether these were alternative names for locks or whether they were the names of stop locks with a single pair of gates to prevent loss of water has still to be discovered.

When I had the privilege of being Chairman of the Canal Trust I once included a story in my column in the Trust's quarterly magazine, The Wharfinger, relating a

Introduction

tale about Christopher Wren (before he was knighted), who liked to make incognito visits to the building site that was to become St. Paul's.

It is said that on one occasion he spoke to a man who was working with a yardstick on a piece of bare earth and asked him what he was doing. "I am a surveyor" the man replied "and I am marking out the course of a great wall". The next man Wren spoke to was chiselling away at a vast piece of stone and Wren asked him the same question. "I'm a Master Mason" he replied, "and I'm shaping the keystone for that soaring arch over yonder. Next Wren spoke to a carpenter who proudly informed him he was preparing one of the great beams which would support the roof of the nave.

Nearby was an elderly woman, bent double over her birch-twig broom sweeping up the shavings the carpenter was making. "And what are you doing, my good woman?" Wren asked. She straightened her back as much as she could and looked him straight in the eye. "Why Sir, I am helping Mr. Wren to build his cathedral."

This book is dedicated to all those incredibly devoted and skilled people who have done (and are doing) so much to make the dream of a canal once again connecting these two ancient cities become a possibility. This may be in the seat of an excavator or a dumper truck, in mud or undergrowth with a spade or slashing hook, surveying, planning and designing projects, at home drowning under the mass of paperwork required to manage the Trust's activities, assets and finances and to secure grant aid, in a committee room late into the night, negotiating with developers, landowners, local authorities and other agencies, representing the Trust at hearings and inquiries, liaising with the media, writing, designing and producing the Trust's own magazine and promotional material, in a hot kitchen making chocolate cakes or leek and potato soup, or on a cold, wet display stand promoting the work of the Trust and selling cuddly toys, draw tickets or even copies of this book to reluctant members of the public.

And, of course, to those who clear up the mess others have made.

Richard Skeet

Hereford and the River Wye

Of the three cities celebrated for the longest running music festival in the world - Hereford, Gloucester and Worcester, Hereford is, by any measure, by far the smallest. The reason for this is as much a matter of simple geography and the effect of that on history than anything else. Gloucester was an important inland port on the River Severn and Worcester was a mere 28 miles upstream. From Gloucester to the open sea at Avonmouth is about 50 miles. The Severn is wide and deep, at least as far as Worcester, and in the 18th and 19th century trows carrying up to 100 tons of cargo were a common sight.

Figure 1: Barges on the Wye at Ross around 1834 showing the varied traffic, both in goods and tourists. Colourised from an engraving by W. Watling (Tim Ward)

By contrast, the Wye is shallow with many twists and turns. In the winter the river is frequently in flood, and in the summer parts of it can be almost dry. From Hereford to the Severn at Beachley Point, nine miles upstream of Avonmouth, is more than 78 difficult miles. The river is tidal for 15 miles, as far as Bigsweir, and larger trows could reach Brockweir Quay assisted by the tide but goods for passage further upstream had to be transferred to small barges with shallower draft.

Such vessels would be limited to a cargo of a mere 20 tons in order to reach Hereford. Timber and bark, for the tanning industry, were the main cargoes downstream and coal from the Forest of Dean comprised most of the upstream traffic. The Wye was reckoned to be navigable for only about 200 days a year which enabled sufficient coal to reach Hereford to satisfy domestic needs, but no more. It is for this reason that Hereford never became an industrialised city like Worcester and Gloucester, its main manufactured goods being gloves and lace making.

There was local traffic in lime and agricultural products, but it was unusual for these to be carried downstream beyond Chepstow. In the years of poor harvests at the end of the 18th century, the passage of trows carrying grain bound for Bristol through Wyeside villages of hungry people gave rise to serious riots and even the theft of their cargo.

Figure 2: Barges on the Wye at Llandogo in 1845 shown in a colourised print of a lithograph by William Bartlett and Thomas Mann (Tim Ward)

Various ambitious plans were developed to improve navigation on the Wye but few were implemented, the exceptions being the construction of flood gates at New Weir, which we now call Symonds Yat, and the construction of the River Wye Horse Towing Path between Lydbrook and Hereford. The first two barges to use the Towing Path, each hauled by two horses, arrived in Hereford in 1811. Even after this it seems that horses were seldom used, the teams of bow haulers retaining their work for many years afterwards and the Wye itself remained much as it is today.

Nevertheless, Hereford depended almost entirely upon the Wye for its commercial transport and both banks of the river were lined with wharves,

Hereford and the River Wye

warehouses, and yards where barges were built. Contemporary maps show a number of the wharves but there is very little evidence of this today, though a small number of warehouses near the old Wye Bridge have survived to be given a new lease of life as residential or business properties.

Figure 3: Part of Cole and Roper's 1806 map of Hereford showing the riverside features. Strangely, Castle Wharf below Castle Green and one of the major wharves, is not shown (Author)

Figure 4: One of the old warehouses below Wye Bridge which now has a new lease of life in the Left Bank Village complex (Author)

In the 17th and 18th centuries every town and village near the Wye had its wharf and many had yards where barges were built. Usually the wharf was just

Hereford and the River Wye

a length of riverbank or barges were simply beached to be unloaded. Stone wharves were a rarity.

Towards the end of the 18th century the entrepreneurs of Hereford were seeing the prosperity brought to the Midlands' towns and cities by the canals built by James Brindley. What Hereford needed was a canal. Not only would a canal to Gloucester be only a little over 30 miles long, saving 80 miles of difficult rivers, it would pass close to the collieries in the north of the Forest of Dean. The Duke of Bridgewater's maxim that *"A navigation should have coals at the heel of it"* was taken as a guarantee that there was money to be made. The days of "canal mania" had arrived and local businesses wanted part of the action.

Figure 5: A Canal Meeting shown in a hand-coloured etching from Isaac Cruikshank, 1797. (British Museum)

Several canal schemes were proposed for Herefordshire. Eighteen miles of the Leominster Canal were built but it failed to reach Hereford, the Severn at Stourport and the border town of Kington as had been planned.

Other proposals included using the Frome valley to Bromyard and Tenbury, a line from Bridgnorth to Ludlow and Leintwardine and the Yazor Valley to Hereford, but they all came to nothing. If a canal between Hereford and Gloucester was to succeed, much better planning was required.

Early Schemes

The first serious plan to build canals in Herefordshire was developed by Brindley's pupil, Robert Whitworth around 1777. Whitworth was a distinguished engineer having worked with both James Brindley and John Smeaton. Whitworth proposed an ambitious route from the Severn at Stourport to Leominster and then to Hereford utilising the River Lugg. From Hereford, the navigation would return to the Severn by way of Ledbury and the Leadon Valley, re-joining the river just above Gloucester. The only part of Whitworth's plan ever to be built was a section between Leominster and the coal mines at Mamble which became the isolated Leominster Canal but it contained some important ideas.

In 1789 Richard Hall proposed a route from Hereford to the Severn via Ledbury joining the river at Wainlodes, about halfway between Tewkesbury and Gloucester, but soon revised it to follow Whitworth's route down the Leadon Valley but with a branch to the coal mines at Newent which would serve the mines which was expected would provide much valuable traffic for the new canal.

On Thursday, March 18th 1790 a meeting was held at which it was agreed to set up a company to build a canal between Hereford and the Severn and a "Committee of the Proprietors of the Herefordshire and Gloucestershire Canal Navigation" was formed. Shares in the Company would cost £100 and Josiah Clowes was appointed Engineer. Clowes was a wise choice. He had worked on the Chester Canal and the Stroudwater Navigation and more recently had worked as Robert Whitworth's assistant on the Thames and Severn Canal and was largely responsible for the construction of the Sapperton Tunnel, 3817 yards long.

Clowes obviously came under pressure from the canal promoters to revise Whitworth's route to take it closer to Newent and the mines at Kilcot and Boulsdon. In a letter to the promoters, no doubt recalling the engineering difficulties experienced in the building of Sapperton Tunnel, he advised as follows:

> "Upon a careful examination of the country from Ledbury to Newent, I find it so much intersected with hills, that it is impracticable to carry the main line by way of Newent. But a lateral branch to Newent may be made as laid down in the plan by Mr. Hall, which in my opinion will answer every requisite purpose."

Early Schemes

The planned route included two tunnels, one in Hereford of 440 yards and a much longer one near Ashperton of 1,320 yards. Aqueducts were required to carry the canal over the rivers Lugg and Frome. The line involved over 20 locks in its 35½ mile course. It was designed to be slightly larger than Brindley's seven-foot gauge narrow canals, to accommodate vessels 70' long and 8' beam. Anyone who has experienced life on a boat of eight-foot beam will know how much more space there seems to be compared with the standard narrow boat. If only all the narrow canals had been built to that slightly larger gauge! As was common practice at the time, Clowes goes on to give a remarkably precise estimate of the cost.

> "I have made my estimate for a canal of proper dimensions for the navigation of vessels 70 feet long and 8 feet wide, which will carry about 35 tons burthen and draw 3 feet 6 inches water. And I particularly recommend the use of these vessels as they such as, from my experience, I have always found to be the best adapted for the dispatch of business on canals."
>
> My calculation, for the execution of the plan, the particulars of which are given in my Estimate, amounts to £69,997 13s 6d."

The various options considered between 1777 and 1796 are shown in Figure 1.

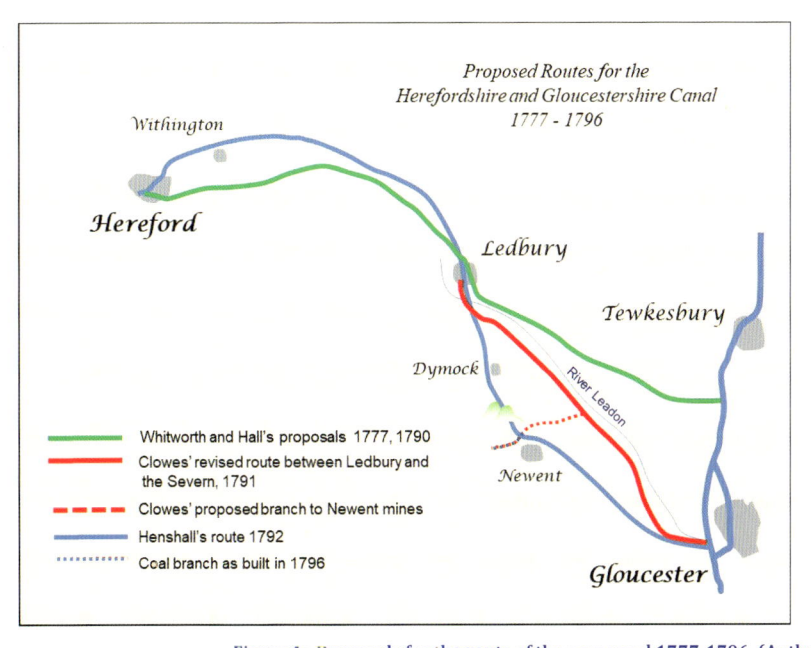

Figure 1: Proposals for the route of the new canal 1777-1796 (Author)

9

Early Schemes

As part of the promotion a series of exquisite fans made of paper and ivory was made for "the ladies of the shareholders" showing the line of the canal. One survives in the Hereford Museum and is shown in Figure 2. In the detail shown in Figure 3 the section from Ledbury to the Severn can be seen clearly, as can the branch to Newent. There is nothing new in sales - "Buy shares in our canal and get a free ladies' fan!"

Figure 2: The promotional fan given to the ladies of the shareholders in the canal (Author)

Figure 3: A Detail of the Promotional Fan showing the branch to the Newent mines (Author)

On March 2nd 1791 a Bill for "Making and maintaining a Navigable Canal from the City of Hereford to the City of Gloucester, with a Collateral Cut from the same to the Town of Newent in the County of Gloucester" was laid before Parliament, though not everyone was impressed.

Protest drawing attention to a dubious business case, inadequate funding and vandalism of the countryside, remarkably reminiscent of the present counter-arguments to HS2, were expressed in petitions considered by the House

Early Schemes

of Commons where *"several Gentlemen, Freeholders, Farmers, and others, Proprietors and Occupiers of Land on or near the line of an intended Navigable Canal"* pleaded;

> "That the Scheme of the said intended Canal is merely speculative, and by no Means ascertained so as to justify the Undertaking, and that the Land in general, through which the said Canal is intended to pass, is very rich Meadow and Pasture Ground, great Part thereof fertilized by the adjacent Streams of Water, which will be either destroyed or rendered useless by the said Canal; and that the Land and Property of several of the Petitioners, from the peculiar Situation thereof, will be more injured and affected by the said Canal than any other Individual having Land on or near the said Line, and all the lands on or near the Line will be considerably lessened in Value, and rendered extremely incommodious in the Cultivation thereof; and that the Line of the said Canal is nearly Central to (and at only a short distance from) the Navigable Rivers Severn and Wye which, it is presumed, are amply sufficient and convenient for the Uses and Purposes of the surrounding Country"
>
> *Journals of the House of Commons Volume 46 p. 254-5, 261*

From Ledbury "Several Gentlemen, Tradesmen, and others" with clear evidence of collusion, had even more to say;

> "That the Scheme of the said intended Canal is entirely speculative, and by no Means ascertained, so as to justify the Undertaking ... and that the Turnpike Tolls of Ledbury aforesaid will be materially lessened, whereby the Securities thereon, amounting at present to £5,000 and upwards, will be greatly injured ; that the Markets and Trade of Ledbury will be wholly lost, and many of the Inhabitants thereof ruined, and the Property of many Land Proprietors and Landholders, on the Line of the intended Canal, will lie greatly injured, particularly so as such Line runs through a very rich Tract of Land, the greater Part whereof is Meadow and Pasture Ground fertilized by the adjacent Streams of Water, which will either be destroyed or rendered useless by the said Canal"
>
> *Ibid*

The gentlemen of Hereford, expressed similar views:

> "... the River Wye flowing through the Centre, and from the one Extremity to the other, of the County of Hereford, will always afford a more speedy, safe, and cheap, Conveyance than the proposed Canal ... the

Early Schemes

> Navigation afforded by the River Wye is more than adequate to all the Purposes which the Trade and Business of the City and Neighbourhood of Hereford require, to which, in every Point of View the proposed Canal appears to the Petitioners not only unnecessary and useless, but likely, in the Effect and Operation, to produce to far the greater Number of the Inhabitants serious Inconveniencies and Mischiefs"

In 1791 the gentlemen of Hereford needn't have worried too much about any serious Inconveniences and Mischiefs. It was to be over half a century before these became a possible threat to the city. The petitioners' view of the Wye seems to be through rather rose-tinted spectacles. Only ten years later William Coxe was writing;

> From Lidbrook large quantities of coal are sent to Ross and Hereford; and we passed several barges towed by ten or eleven men, which by great exertions are drawn to Hereford in two days ... these barges "on account of the shoals do not draw more than five or six inches of water."
> Coxe, William, *An Historical Tour of in Monmouthshire (1801) p. 253*

These barges could hardly have carried a great tonnage of cargo, but the gentlemen of Hereford also expressed views about the quality of the coal from the Newent mines:

> ... the Petitioners apprehend, in case a Colliery should be established at Newent, the Coals to be produced there are of a Quality so very indifferent and bad, as to be unfit for general Use, and that they cannot be rendered to the Inhabitants of the City and Neighbourhood of Hereford, cheaper than those of the Forest of Dean Coals of an unexceptionable Quality, which always have, and now do, abundantly supply the Inhabitants of the City and Neighbourhood of Hereford by the Barges and other Craft navigating the River Wye;

The concerns about both the quality and quantity of the coal from Newent and the total inadequacy of the financial arrangements turned out to be very close to the truth. No doubt by the turn of the century the words "I told you so" were often being heard in the market places of Hereford and Ledbury. There were, however, several (much briefer!) supportive petitions from Hereford, the market towns, several villages and from places as far away as Brecon and Hay-on-Wye. The Bill received its second reading on March 7th with 61 "Yeas" and five "Noes". The Act received Royal Assent on April 17th 1791.

Early Schemes

Clearly the promotional propaganda was effective as by 1792 the finance authorised by the Act had been raised and engineering work began, starting from the Gloucester end. But the Proprietors, clearly disappointed that Clowes had followed Whitworth's route, were concerned that the canal did not pass close enough to the mines at Newent, on which so much depended.

They commissioned Hugh Henshall, Brindley's assistant and son-in-law to re-survey the line between Ledbury and Gloucester. Henshall, who also had considerable experience of building canal tunnels, but now perhaps under some pressure, told them what they wanted to hear – that taking the route via Newent tunnelling under the hills north of Oxenhall was not as impracticable as Clowes believed.

Meeting in the Swan Inn, Hereford, on the 8th of October 1792 the Committee made the fatal decision to recommend to the General Meeting that Henshall's revised line be adopted.

> Mr Henshall's Report having been read agreed that it be recommended to the General Meeting to be held tomorrow, that the Work is immediately begun at Gloucester, Ledbury and at both ends of the tunnel on the Summit pound as pointed out in Mr. Henshall's Report and that the variation and extension of the line pointed out by Mr. Henshall be also recommended. In consequence of Mr. Henshall's Report we are of the opinion that it will not be advisable to make the canal on a reduced scale.
>
> *Company Minute Books: October 8th 1792*

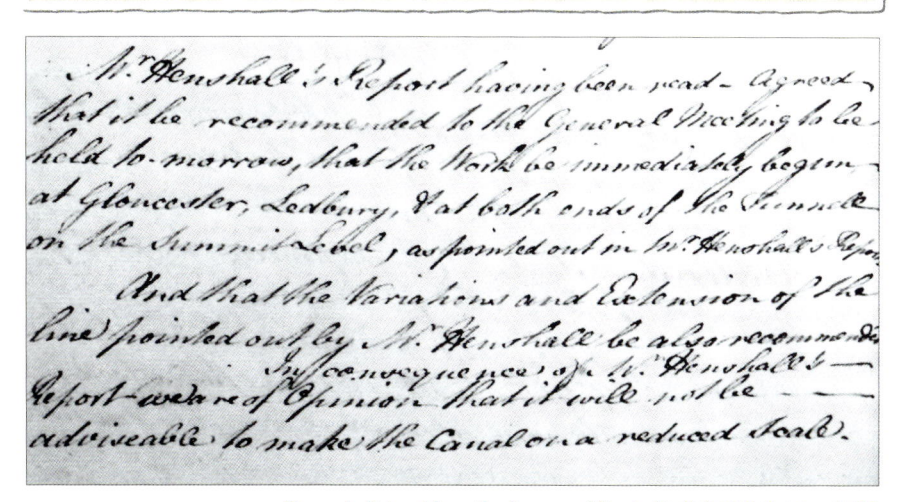

Figure 4: Extract from the Company Minute Book for 8th October 1792

Early Schemes

Though it was only when construction beyond Newent began that the dire effect of this change to the route became apparent. Such was the importance of this resolution that the complete minute is reproduced in Figure 4. But the die was cast and the Company was never truly to recover from this decision. On February 22nd 1793 Parliament heard the first reading of a Bill to alter the line of the canal from the route prescribed in the 1791 Act. The critical amendment read:

> "...and that an Alteration in the Line of the said Canal, from or near Tilley's Green, in the Parish of Dymock, in the County of Gloucester, to or near to, Barbers Bridge, in the same County, so as to carry the Line of the said Canal through Newent, will not only render any Collateral Cut unnecessary, and thereby save many Acres of valuable Land from being taken for the Use of the said Canal, but will also be of great Advantage to the Counties of Hereford and Gloucester, and of public Utility, in as much as such Line will pass through a Country abounding with Coal and Lime Stone;"

The new Bill also provided for the line of the canal to be extended at the Hereford end from Widemarsh to Bysters Gate, closer to the city centre, which must have caused even greater anxiety on the part of those concerned about the serious Inconveniences and Mischiefs. It also contained provision for the canal company to exploit any coal deposits discovered during the construction of the canal.

It is likely that Henshall and Clowes had together reconsidered the Newent route and the long tunnel which would be necessary. They were old friends, Henshall having been a witness at Clowes' wedding in 1762. Clowes was probably the most experienced canal tunnel engineer in the country having worked on some of the longest built at that time, including Sapperton, Dudley and Lappal.

During the Committee stage it was Clowes himself who gave evidence in support of the revised route:

> "Mr. Josiah Clowes, an Engineer, being examined, said, That Surveys and Levels have been taken, to ascertain the Practicability of making the Deviations and Extension before-mentioned, and as described in the Petition, and the same are found to be highly practicable and eligible."
>
> *Journals of the House of Commons Volume 48 page 454*

Clearly Clowes had changed his mind about the difficulties of the Newent route

Early Schemes

- or had had it changed for him. Parliament accepted his evidence, ordered the Bill to read a third time and went on to debate a more important matter, namely the duty on beer costing more than six shillings a barrel.

Some months before, the Company had already begun organising the construction of the canal:

> Ordered - that a Workshop for the Carpenters and Wheelbarrow Makers be immediately built in the Ground adjoining Leaden between Over Mill and Vineyard Hill.
> *Company Committee Minute Books: November 8th 1792*

With the provision of wheelbarrows in place, the Company began to look for contractors.

> Ordered - That Advertisements be inserted into the Hereford, Gloucester, Worcester and Birmingham Papers for Persons to contract for cutting the Canal and forming the Towing Path through that part of the parishes of Lassington and Rudford where the line is set out..

By December the Company was ready to set up its office in Gloucester, prior to which the Committee had met at the Bell Inn and the George Coffee House in Gloucester and at the Swan Inn in Hereford:

> Agreed with Mr. Paul Walker to take his house late in the occupation of Mr. Greatwood on Foreign Bridge in Gloucester from Christmas next for the use of a Clerk and the Committee at £20 per annum rent. Ordered - that necessary furniture by provided by Mr. Price for the above house, and that a Board with the Words "Herefordshire and Gloucestershire Canal Navigation Office" painted thereon be placed over the Door of the said House.
> *Company Committee Minute Books: December 6th 1792*

Having agreed their new headquarters, the Committee got down to organising the first part of the canal to be cut - The Hereford and Gloucester Canal was on its way.

Gloucester to Ledbury

Work along the level section of the canal between the junction with the Severn and Rudford began well enough. Clowes' original plan took the canal over the Western Channel of the Severn on an aqueduct and across Alney Island before locking into the Severn River's Eastern Channel a short distance above Gloucester Docks.

The idea of an aqueduct did not go down at all well with the local landowners who could see this as a likely cause of damaging flooding if the flow of the river was obstructed. The plan was changed to cross the Western Channel on the level. The linking channel was excavated in 1793 using an earth-moving machine patented by the engineer John Carne in 1784.

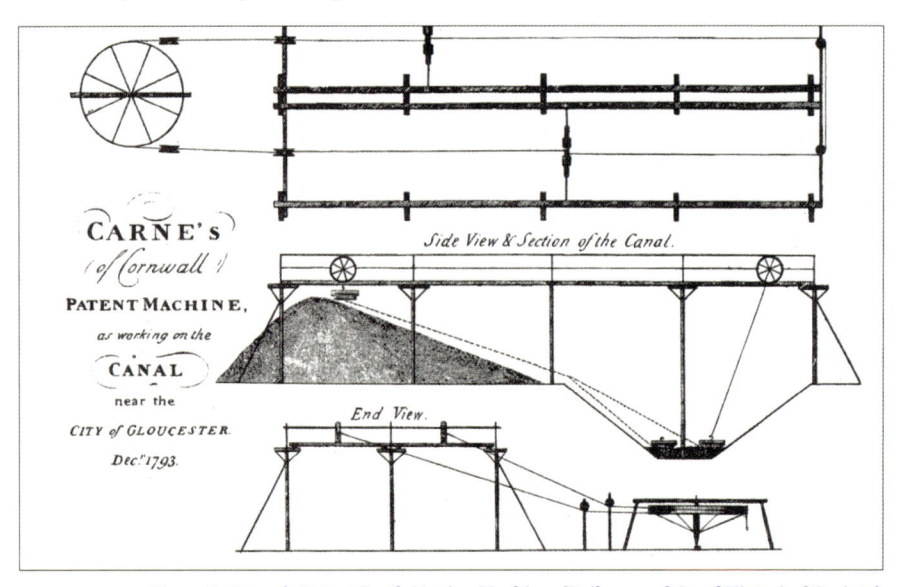

Figure 1: Carne's Patent Earth Moving Machine (Railway and Canal Historical Society)

It is not altogether clear from the drawing how the machine worked. Possibly this was a deliberate ploy on Carne's part to prevent others copying his ideas!

Under the direction of Peter Cross-Rudkin a working model was recently built at Coventry University. It took several attempts before a successful working machine could be made and it is possible that the bucket was filled by navvies and the machine was just used to dispose of the spoil. Almost certainly the machine was not quite as useful as it was cracked up to be. We know only that it was used on Alney Island and at Dymock and though Carne was involved with other canals there is little evidence that his machine was used elsewhere.

Figure 2: A One-tenth scale working model of Carne's Patent Earth-moving Machine

> Ordered – That William Maysey be employed as a Clerk or Superintendent of the works; to be allowed a Salary after the rate of 50 Guineas per annum, & the use of Apartments in the House taken of Mr. Walker – Also to provide him Fire & Candles, & to allow him his travelling expenses whenever he is sent from home or the Canal concern – his time to commence from 1st December instant.
>
> *Company Committee Minute Books: December 12th 1792*

Excavation and building of the canal between Over and Newent was going well including the construction of the 11 locks. Clowes supervised the building process but, as he was involved with half a dozen other canal projects, he could hardly have devoted much time to it and William Maysey was appointed to take day to day charge of operations, a position he held for the next 30 years. Work was also in progress between Dymock and the northern end of the long Oxenhall Tunnel and Carne's machine was moved to work here. Work also began on the tunnel and cuttings beyond Ledbury at Ashperton.

While all of this work was going on the Company was also getting side-tracked into speculative mining operations around Newent. Small deposits of poor-quality coal were found but this only seemed to encourage further explorations. The details of these operations need not be retold here, suffice to say that far too much of the available capital was wasted in the vain hope of finding sufficient deposits which would justify the expense of the canal.

In December 1794 Clowes died at his home at Middlewich at the age of 59 and Robert Whitworth returned to Gloucestershire to take his place as engineer with the responsibility of driving a canal through a landscape he himself had thought it better to avoid.

Figure 3: Share Certificate No. 116, issued to Samuel Carless in 1793 (Nigel Jefferies)

By the end of October 1795, the canal was open from Over to Oxenhall, a distance of seven miles, which, given the number of locks and bridges constructed, was no small achievement. Work had also progressed on the Oxenhall Tunnel but Whitworth's and Clowes initial reluctance to take this route was beginning to be fully justified. Springs in the hill regularly flooded the workings and it was necessary to install two steam engines to pump the water out and allow work to continue. Much of the tunnel had to be bored through solid rock. By 1797 nearly a third of the projected cost of the whole canal had now been spent on this tunnel alone.

Further capital was raised and at last, in March 1798, the work was completed. John Phillips, probably quoting the Hereford Journal, describes the opening of the canal in some detail:

> "The Herefordshire and Gloucestershire canal from Gloucester to Ledbury is complete! "The opening of this navigation took place on the 30th of March, when several of the proprietors and gentlemen of the committee, embarked at the junction of the coal branch near Newent, in the first vessel freighted with merchandise consigned to Ledbury, which was followed by three others laden with coal. They passed through the Tunnel at Oxenhall which is 2192 yards in length, in the space of 52 minutes, and were met at the extremity by several gentlemen, and entertained with a cold collation at the Boyce, the seat of Mr. Moggeridge, one of the proprietors of the valuable coal mines recently opened at Oxenhall.
>
> Both ends of the tunnel, as well as the banks of the canal, were lined with spectators, who hailed the boats with reiterated acclamations. It is supposed that upwards of 2000 persons were present on their arrival at Ledbury, (about 9 miles) which they reached in 4 hours. A dinner was provided on the occasion, at the George inn, where the greatest conviviality prevailed, and many appropriate toasts were drank. The advantages which must result from this inland navigation to Ledbury and the adjoining country are incalculable. In the article of coal, the inhabitants of this district will reap an important benefit by the immediate reduction in price of at least 10s.per ton. Coals of the first quality are now delivered at the wharf, close to Ledbury, at 13s/6d whereas the former price was 24s per ton.
>
> *Phillips, John: A General History of Inland Navigation 4th edition 1803 p. 587-*

The population of Ledbury at the time was little more than 3,000 and it seems unlikely that two thirds of these turned out to cheer the arrival of the first boats to reach the town.

It is also improbable that this "first quality" coal came from the Newent pits. Far more likely, it was coal shipped up the Severn from Lydney. Indeed, now that coal could reach Ledbury from far afield it reduced the need to rely on local coal from Newent.

Proposed Canal Routes to Herefordshire 1777

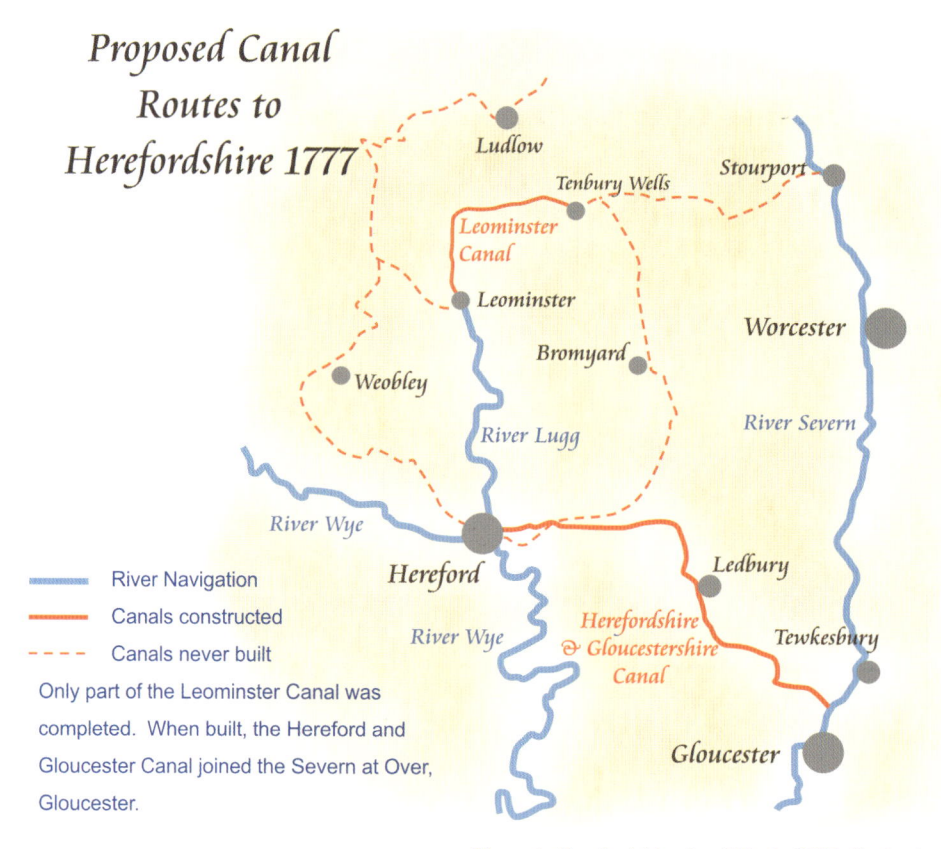

- ▬▬ River Navigation
- ▬▬ Canals constructed
- ---- Canals never built

Only part of the Leominster Canal was completed. When built, the Hereford and Gloucester Canal joined the Severn at Over, Gloucester.

Figure 4: Herefordshire Canal Mania 1777 (Author)

There were now problems in Gloucester. The cut across Alney Island was suffering badly from the silt brought up by the tide and Whitworth began building a dam across the Severn at Over to prevent this. Understandably, the local landowners were more upset about this than they had been about the aqueduct and the Company was ordered to remove it.

The wharf at Ledbury was located on the Ross Road still a mile from the town centre. The only evidence of it now is the Wharf House which has been preserved, albeit much altered from its original form.

Figure 5: The former wharf house at Ledbury wharf

And so things stood for nearly half a century. Despite costing far more than the estimate for the whole project, the canal was only half built. Hereford was still some 16 miles away. Because the main source of water, the had not been reached there was a chronic shortage of water, at least on the section between Ledbury and Newent.

The "valuable coal mines at Oxenhall" proved as disappointing as all the others. A short branch had been built to serve them, leaving the main line above the top lock near the village. Soon after 1800, traffic along this branch ceased altogether.

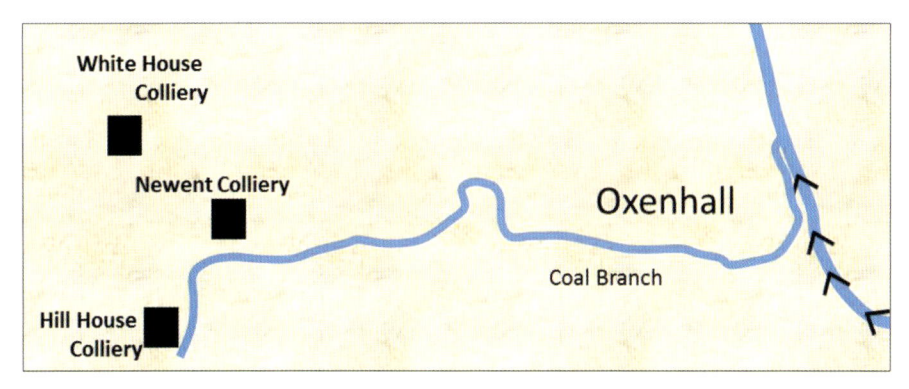

Figure 6: The Coal branch around 1800

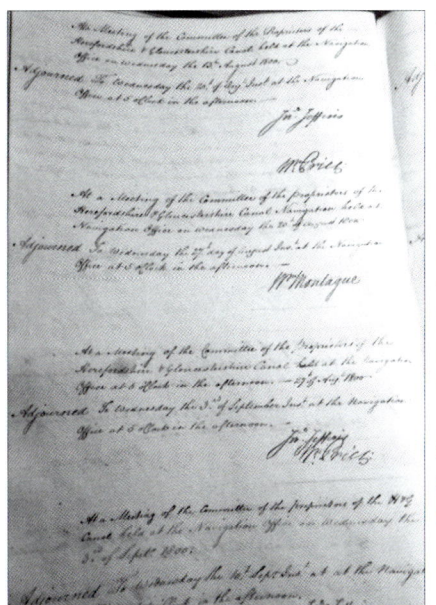

The canal was operated by a minimum of staff and it appears that the Committee never actually met between 1800 and 1812 the minutes simply recording a series of adjournments.

In 1812 the Committee did get round to having a meeting – no doubt much to the relief of lock keeper Thomas Hatchett who was able to point out that he had not been properly paid for the last 13 years.

Figure 7: The Company minute book for the Summer of 1800. It appears that the meetings were inquorate and so were automatically adjourned.

Table of Tolls 1791

For coal, two-pence per ton per mile.

For dung and other manure, bricks, lime-stone, and other stone (except block-stone), and clay, one penny per ton per mile.

For corn, grain, meal, etc. (except hops and wool), from Hereford, or from Ledbury to the junction with the Severn, three shillings and sixpence per ton.

For the same goods from any other part of the canal or collateral cut, to the Severn, two-pence halfpenny per ton per mile.

For corn, grain, meal, block-stone, hops, wool, etc. not specified, three-pence per ton per mile.

Goods passing between Hereford and Ledbury pay tonnage for half a mile less than the actual distance.

― ― ― ❖❖❖ ― ― ―

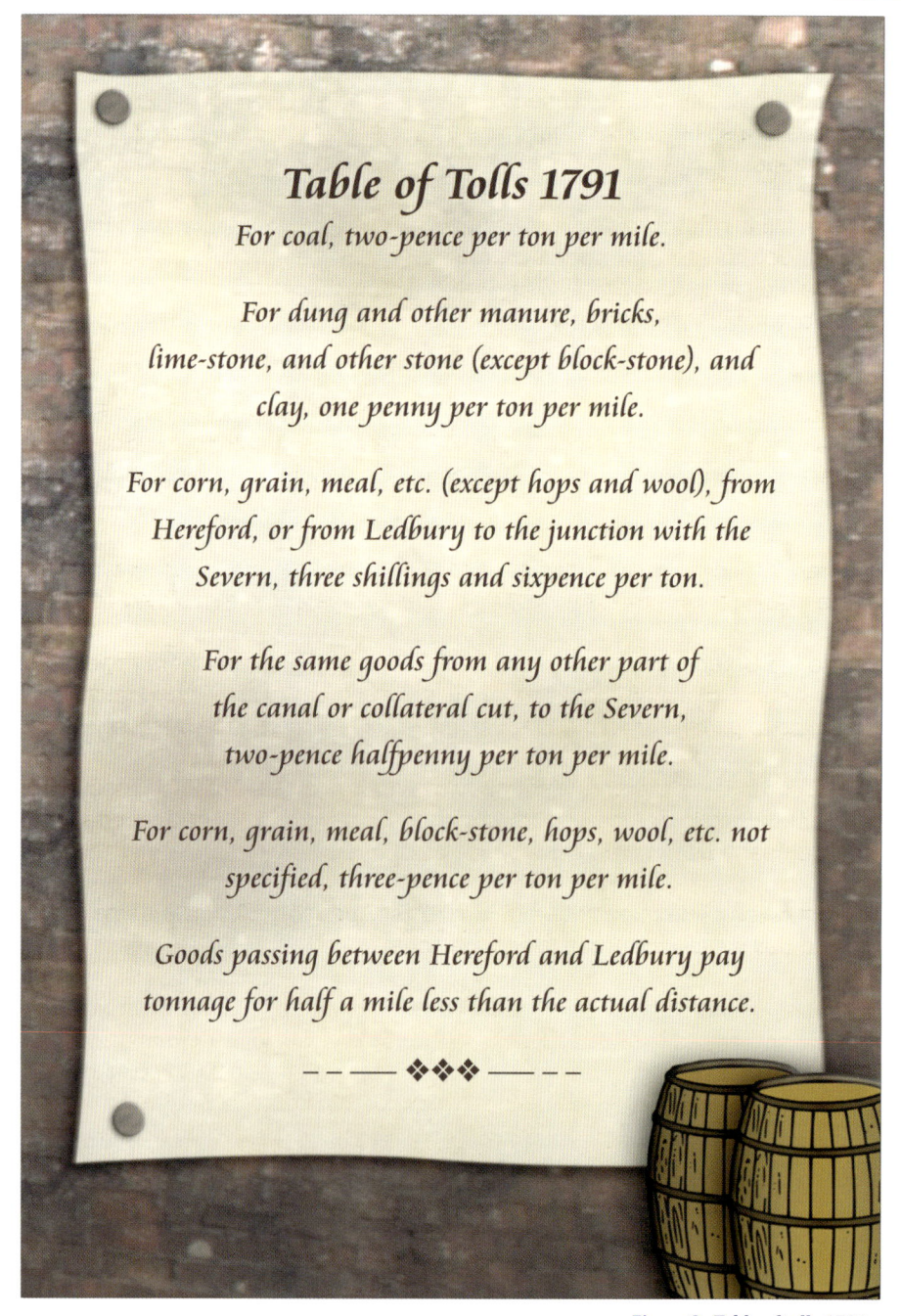

Figure 8: Table of tolls 1791

Mr. Hatchett had been appointed in April 1798 as Wharfinger at Newent at an annual salary of 26 guineas and must have also been given the job as a lock-keeper.

Tolls were to be charged according to a rather complicated formula specified before the canal opened. Presumably tolls between Hereford and Ledbury did not apply! See Figure 8 opposite.

> Tho's Hatchett having applied for some remuneration for attendance as Lockkeeper for thirteen years last, it was resolved that he be paid Twenty Pounds on that account, & that his wages in future shall be as such as Wharfinger & Lock-Keeper.
> *Company Committee Minute Books: November 12th 1812*

The canal received a boost to its trade in 1810 when the 2nd Baron Somers began the building of Eastnor Castle. 4,000 tons of sandstone, quarried in the Forest of Dean were transported by canal to Ledbury and thence by mule to the castle.

There were some half-hearted attempts to improve the water supply but there were insufficient funds to carry out the work necessary to reach the Frome.

While the Company employed lock-keepers and lengthsmen there appears to have been no accommodation provided for them and, if Mr. Hatchett is anything to go by, sometimes their employees had more than one job.

It is clear that the Company was being run on a shoestring. This meeting in 1812 seems to signal the first signs of recovery and Maysey had reported that the Company was in credit to the tune of £1,200.

The minutes of the Committee held on 21st April 1814 illustrate some of the day-to-day issues faced in running the canal.

> It appearing that considerable damage has been done to the works by boats passing through the Locks in the night. Resolved, That measures be taken to prevent the passing of boats between the hours of seven in the evening and five in the morning during the Summer months and between five in the evening and seven in the morning during the winter except at the time of Spring Tides.
>
> Mr. Maysey states that about 20 oak trees of about 15 inches girth will be wanting for Lock gates. Ordered, that he take proper means to procure the same. It being represented that the Bridge, called Yewtree Bridge in the Tything of Malswick in the Parish of Newent is, at present, in a very

> inconvenient and dangerous state. Ordered, that Mr. Maysey examine the site of it with accuracy and report to the Committee what would be the expense of raising the parapet walls and Coping of the same, and improving the approach to the bridge by lessening the declivity.
>
> *Company Committee Minute Books: April 21st 1814*

By June 1817 the Company felt confident enough to contemplate extending the canal:

> Resolved, that Mr. Ralph Walker be employed as Engineer to survey the line of Canal from Moat Meadow to Monkhide Mill immediately, and, estimate the expense thereof or in case he shall be engaged, that his Nephew Mr. J Walker, or other competent Person be applied to for the same Purpose"
>
> *Company Committee Minute Books: June 11th 1817*

Mr Ralph Walker was not otherwise engaged and was appointed as engineer, though nothing seems to have been done about the extension and in August the Committee ordered that "the canal from Ledbury to Over be thoroughly repaired" and to "obtain an estimate for the expense of making a wharf at Over with a house for the Clerk." The Committee approved the building of the house in the following January.

Ralph Walker was not without stature as a civil engineer, having worked with John Rennie and William Jessop in the building of the East India and Surrey Commercial Docks in London, but there is no record of him actually designing anything for the Hereford and Gloucester Canal. He died in 1824.

After not meeting for six years, on May 13th 1827, meeting at the Feathers Hotel in Ledbury with John Biddulph in the Chair, the Committee now had an important decision to make. William Maysey had been suffering from cancer for some while and was asking to be allowed to retire. The Committee granted this request and made the extraordinary decision to appoint as his successor a local man of 23 years of age.

> Resolved, That Mr. Stephen Ballard be appointed as such upon at a salary of £60 a year, up to the 1st of January 1828 untill which time the present clerk shall continue his salary and appointment on condition that he renders every possible assistance and affords the requisite information to his successor.
>
> *Company Committee Minute Books May 19th 1827*

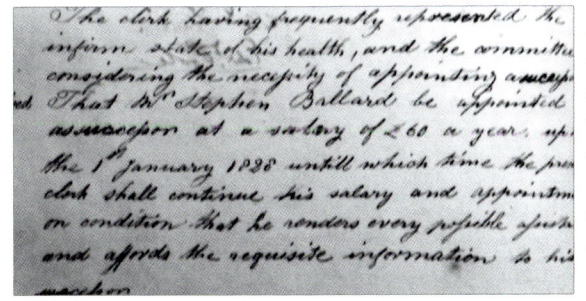

Figure 9: The Company minute recording the decision to appoint Stephen Ballard as clerk.

John Biddulph was the owner of Ledbury Park and of land through which the canal ran and it was almost certainly Biddulph who persuaded the Committee in August to appoint a bright young man from Malvern Link as Company Clerk to succeed William Maysey.

Stephen Ballard had a great interest in horticulture and geometry, but without sufficient capital to fulfil his dream of starting his own company.

Frustrated by this, he had turned to the building trade and for two years was apprenticed to a Cheltenham Builder, Henry Lucy, working mostly as a carpenter. When Lucy went out of business the far-sighted Biddulph, perhaps knowing something of Ballard's talents, grasped the opportunity this presented.

The appointment of a man of 23 with no experience at all of transport management or engineering to this post looks like another disastrous decision on the part of the Company, but it was undoubtedly the best choice it ever made. He was given a salary of £60 per annum "with house and travelling expenses".

From the outset Ballard believed that the only future for the canal lay in its extension to Hereford. Apart from the increase in trade, the extension was needed to secure an adequate water supply for the rest of the canal. In 1828 he was given a £20 bonus for his "zeal and activity" and particularly for his plans, in which he was assisted by the young Robert Stephenson, to bring a water supply from Canon Frome Mill. Ironically, this scheme was never implemented. If it had been it would have been the first seven miles of the canal to Hereford.

Ballard used the first years with the Company well. There being little need for his services on a day-to-day basis he travelled widely, visiting the Shropshire and Ellesmere Canals and the canals around Manchester. He made copious notes and sketches, no doubt all the while planning the completion of his own canal.

By 1830 the argument seems to have been won and the Company was buying land to complete the canal to Hereford. By September Ballard was able to report to the committee:

> I beg leave to inform you that the new Lock at the Wharf is complete excepting the gates, that the new cutting as far as the Little Marcle Road is completed and that the Bridge to carry the Little Marcle road over the canal is now in progress.
>
> Ballard, Stephen: Letter to the Committee :September 2nd 1830

In December 1831 Ballard reported that up to 1827 the canal had to close for three or four months every year through lack of water, but supplies had been improved and since then the only stoppage had been for six weeks that summer. At Ledbury, there was now:

> ...on the Wharf an excellent carpenters workshop, a Warehouse, a Stable a drying shed for timber, and inclosed timber yard, the machine house is enlarged and now contains six rooms and a new bason has been made which is a great convenience to the traders in unloading their Coal.
>
> Ballard, Stephen: Diary entry for September 30th 1838

Figure 10: The Canal at Ledbury Gasworks - a charming, if not wholly accurate sketch
(from a private collection)

Gloucester to Ledbury

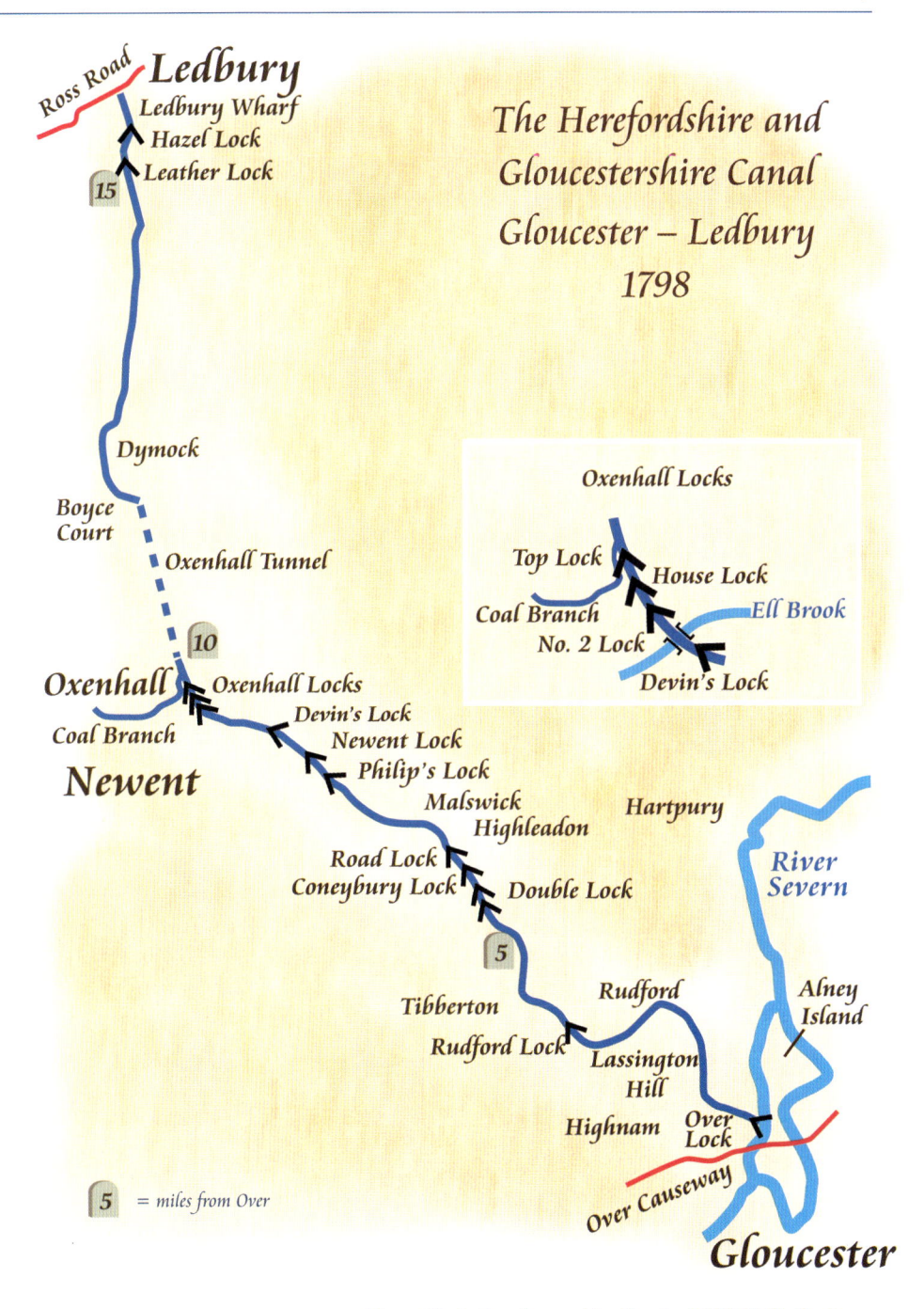

Figure 11: Options for reaching Hereford, 1837-8 (Author)

The Ledbury wharf had also been enlarged and several locks had been fitted with new gates. The average income had risen from £552 per annum prior to 1827 to £1,452 since.

On May 20th 1832, with 27 tons of stone aboard, the canal's repair boat passed through the wharf lock to the stone yard above, and probably to the gas works beyond the Little Marcle Road, but the canal was extended no further.

In 1837 Ballard began to prepare plans in earnest, making revisions to the route authorised by Parliament in 1793. These revisions required a further Act, but this would also enable further capital to be raised. The estimated cost of completion now stood at £75,000. Various alternative routes into Hereford were considered including locking into the Wye below Hereford to save costs.

Another proposed using the Lugg with the optimistic thought of traffic from the Leominster Canal. The various options are shown in Figure 11.

Ballard had been referred to as "Clerk and Engineer" since early in 1832, but in 1838 the Committee called upon James Walker, the late Ralph Walker's nephew and President of the Institution of Civil Engineers, to advise them on the route of the proposed extension to Hereford.

Ballard had already explored a number of options and on Saturday September 28th, after breakfast with Walker at the Gloucester Canal Office, drove to Priors Court and together they walked thence along the line to Hereford. Ballard coped better than Walker –

> At Hereford with Mr. Walker, slept at the Green Dragon. Went to a barber's shop and shaved myself. It is a disagreeable thing to be in a strange town on Sunday with no one to speak to and nothing to do, I do not mind being the country by myself. 8 o'clock and Mr Walker not up yet.
>
> *Ballard, Stephen: Diary entry for September 30th 1888*

I don't think Stephen Ballard and James Walker got on particularly well, a couple of weeks later he writes *"Called on Mr. Walker, did not like his behaviour"*

Ballard's strong preference was for the route through the Frome Valley, but on October 1st Walker was called before the Committee and persuaded it to go with the line authorised by Parliament in 1793, but incorporating some of Ballard's suggestions. The River Lugg option was probably only considered because it is possible that the Leominster Canal Company was prepared to contribute to the cost of improving the Lugg. Their canal had only been opened between Leominster and Mamble the year before and the company was already considering making their connection with the Severn via a tramway instead of canal.

Ballard's time was now being spent in surveying the line of the extension to Hereford, but he was also surveying the River Lugg, no doubt with a view of a possible connection with the canal. He was also working on a flood protection scheme for the Wye below Hereford and on a scheme for the Bishop of Hereford's length of river bank in the palace gardens. Furthermore, he was also working for the Llanelly Railway, with which he was less than impressed, as his diary reveals:

> At Office work of Lugg Survey. Received £50 through Mr. B from the Llanelly Railway company which sum I agreed to take instead of £79, the amount of my bill. I hope the lesson I have learned from the rascals comprising this committee will be of service to me in making any agreement with any other Committee or Company, for I have been used by them in a most shameful manner.
> Ballard, Stephen: Diary entry for May 3rd 1838

A new Bill for the extension of the canal was laid before Parliament on February 20th 1839. Its passage was not entirely straightforward. Ballard records an early difficulty in his diary:

> Hubert Edy went to the House of Commons, he said Lord Shaftesbury opposed the Act. The old arbitrary rascal would give no reason for this unreasonable proceeding and we were informed that there would be no chance of success if we were to attempt to get an act passed without his approval. Thus, it is this one man, an hereditary legislator, has the power to stop a public work without assigning any reason for it.
> Ballard, Stephen: Diary entry for February 20th 1839

The old arbitrary rascal, the father of the great reformer for whom Ballard would have had the highest regard, must have been won around, for the Bill then suffered a slight technical hitch at its Select Committee stage when it was reported that, although the Bill related to the whole length of the canal, no advertisement had been placed in a Gloucester newspaper. However, as the money to be raised under the Act was to be used for works exclusively in Herefordshire and two advertisements had been placed in "a Hereford paper", the Hereford and Gloucester Times, the Bill was allowed to proceed subject to "giving Notices forthwith for three successive weeks in some newspaper of the county of Gloucester".

This achieved, a new Act was obtained on May 31st 1839 authorising the raising of £50,000 by mortgage and £45,000 by shares. It appears that there were no objections from the Gentlemen of Hereford this time – they probably thought it would never happen.

Ballard was now spending much of his time negotiating with landowners, an experience he did not enjoy. He found many of them unreasonable:

> If the whole of an engineer's work was as disagreeable as arranging with landowners, I should not follow up the business. Nothing satisfies them.
>
> *Ballard, Stephen: Diary entry for December 4th 1839*

The Company published a glowing prospectus waxing lyrically on the anticipated income once Hereford had been reached. It proposed that a link to the Leominster Canal could be "effected at trifling expense" yielding an annual income of at least £8,000 and even suggested a seven-mile branch to Bromyard "is very probable, a cursory survey showing that there are no apparent difficulties"

The anonymous writer of "Hints of Ledbury" as far back as 1831 tells us that:

> The advantages that will accrue from completion of the canal to Hereford are great. The deficiency of water, that fatal obstacle, will be supplied from many and permanent sources, whereby constant traffic on the canal will be afforded hitherto so limited, and that to the most unfavourable part of the year. The communication with Hereford will cause a vast addition of business, and the heavy goods of all kinds to and from Ledbury, will be conveyed at probably one half of the present rates of carriage.
>
> *A Native inhabitant (of Ledbury): Hints of Ledbury 1831 pp 97-103*

And so it goes on for several pages. The writer even points to a bit of tax avoidance:

> Every article excepting coal, paid a turnpike toll before it reached the town. By the canal coming within the borough, that tax will be avoided.
>
> *Ibid.*

If the Herefordshire and Gloucestershire Canal could have been built and operated on optimism alone it would surely have been one of the most successful in the country!

But, thanks largely to the enterprise and sheer hard work of Stephen Ballard and a new Committee which consisted entirely of local men, most of whom lived in or around Ledbury, the canal was about to enter a new phase of its history.

Ledbury to Hereford

Before the end of 1839 there was work going on at several places along the canal and Ballard saw his first glimpse of the excavations. His diary records on December 17th:

> "Went to Furnimore where the men were to start this morning on the first contract. The first I saw of the workmen was through a gap in the hedge, they were in the distance and I must say the appearance of them had an electrical effect on me, never shall I forget it. The appearance of the men at work seems to have made a lasting impression on my memory for I almost fancy I can see them now. They were got in a muddle and had lost much labour."
>
> Ballard, Stephen: Diary entry for Dec. 17th 1839

1840 the four deep locks taking the canal from above the wharf lock outside the town were constructed and a new Ledbury Wharf built on or near Bye Street. George Wargent, writing in 1905 recalled:

> "When the Canal started there seemed to be a need for a public house near Bye Street Bridge and the present lodging house was licensed and a big trade was done among the canal people...
>
> "Directly after the canal to Hereford was made Mr Thomas Edy had Bridge House built, and it was known for some years as the 'The Bridge Inn' kept by Thomas Greenway and subsequently by Mr Goode during whose tenancy the licence was lost. A bowling-alley was attached to this inn as to many others in the town."
>
> Wargent, George: Recollections of Ledbury. A series of personal articles written for the Ledbury Free Press & Hereford Advertiser. Reproduced by permission of the Ledbury & District Society Trust.

Figure 1: The former Bridge Inn in Bye Street, Ledbury

Ballard's diary records that by April 1840 there were 500 men working on the canal and he himself was working from dawn to dusk:

> "Commenced work on the Canal soon after 4am. and was tired by breakfast time but was hard at it until 9pm. S. Willcox was so tired that he had to remain at Ashperton"
>
> Ballard, Stephen: Diary entry for May 28th 1840

The first coal arrived at Bye Street on 22nd February 1841, observed by the Committee and an audience of local people.

> "At three o'clock the Committee went to the locks where a great many people had assembled to see the first boat load of coal come into Ledbury at the Bye Street Bridge. Sir J. Mony made a short speech"
>
> Ballard, Stephen: Diary entry for Feb 22nd 1841

Figure 2: The New Wharf, Ledbury (from a private collection)

The census carried out on June 6th that year tells us that Richard Maddox, a Trustee of the new Methodist Chapel in the Homend, was already living at the Wharf doing his accounting. By this time work was well advanced between Ledbury and the tunnel at Ashperton. Ballard had reduced Clowes' planned length of the tunnel itself by 920 yards to a mere 400 by making long, and quite spectacular cuttings, but the work was difficult and, like Oxenhall, required the use of gunpowder in some places. The tunnel was fully lined to provide stability and to keep spring water out. It also included a towpath – an unusual luxury. It was generally known at the time as "Walsopthorne Tunnel" because it was rather closer to the manor house of that name than to Ashperton village.

1841 had been a busy year. On New Year's Eve Stephen Ballard writes:

> "This year I have been very much engaged. Not a single day, not even Sundays have I been disengaged from the work of the Canal. To look back to this time last year it appears an immense long time"
>
> *Ballard, Stephen: Diary entry for Dec 31st 1841*

In 1842 the canal reached Canon Frome and on January 10th agreement was reached with John Hopton of Canon Frome Court for the right to use all the water that flowed over a newly constructed weir and thence to the canal by a long feeder. This was a major achievement, virtually guaranteeing an adequate water supply to the canal all the year round. The Canon Frome Wharf received its first goods the following year with, according to the Hereford Journal, salutary implications for the River Wye:

> HEREFORD and GLOUCESTER CANAL.—On Wednesday last the spirited carriers Messrs. Bunting and Gibson, had their first boat-load of goods to Canon Frome Wharf. From that day may be dated the desertion of the river Wye as a navigation for the conveyance of foreign produce; the opening of the Berkely Canal in 1837 and now the extension of the Hereford and Gloucester Canal to ten miles of Hereford, have given facilities that will, probably, for ever supersede the Wye as a navigation for the carriage of Bristol goods. It must be highly gratifying to the promoters of the canal to find their calculations of traffic are being fully borne out; and, in some instances sources of revenue have already sprang up that were not expected.
>
> *Hereford Journal Jan 11th 1843*

By 1842 there must have been sufficient traffic for there to be queues at the locks, necessitating the Committee to have "the following notice printed and delivered to the Lockkeepers and Traders on the Canal".

> Lockkeepers are directed to see that Boats carrying Grocery and other goods on regular days are not hindered in passing locks and that all other Boats give way and wait at the discretion of the Lockkeepers to allow such regular carrying boats to pass first.
>
> *Company Minute Books, October 24th 1842*

The length of canal between Canon Frome included the crossing of a minor road at Monkhide. Here, the lane crossed at an angle of 60° and the normal practice in such cases would be to slightly re-route the lane to cross at approximately right angles. But Ballard almost always preferred to leave the line of the road unchanged and in this case to build a skew bridge across it. Ballard's bridge is probable the "skewest" brick-built bridge on the entire canal network and demonstrates not only his skill as an engineer but the art of bricklayers working under him. The construction did not go entirely smoothly as a number of cracks appeared when the centring props were removed.

> There were so many props we could not let down the arch regularly, only a part at a time, this caused cracks which much alarmed me.
>
> *Ballard, Stephen: Diary entry for December 2nd 1842.*

Adjustments to loading of the bridge were made and eventually Ballard was satisfied with the result. The bridge still stands today, a Grade II listed building carrying traffic of much heavier vehicles than the engineer could have imagined.

Figure 3: Skew Bridge, Monkhide

By 1844 a regular freight service was running between Ledbury and Birmingham using the Hereford and Gloucester Canal, the River Severn and the Worcester and Birmingham Canal.

Ledbury to Hereford

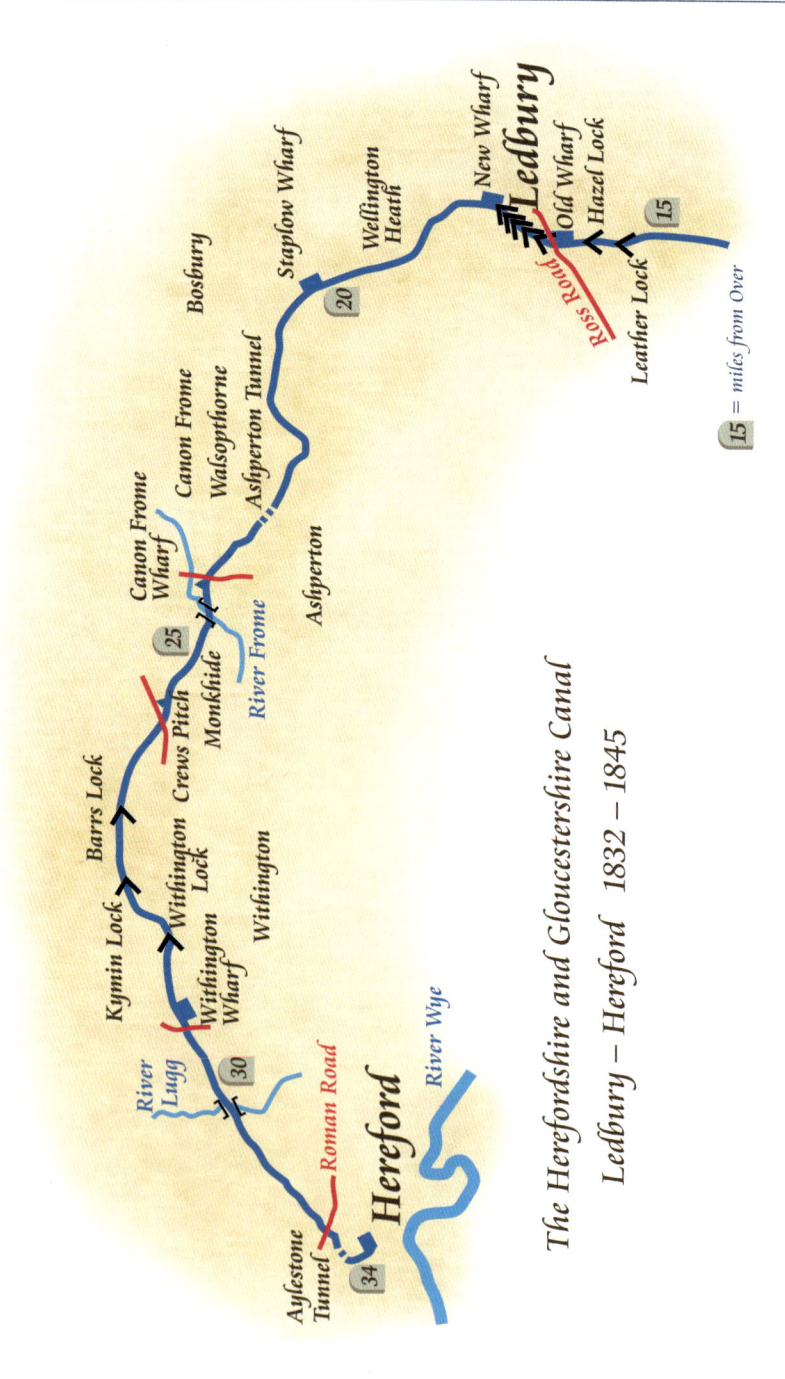

Figure 4: The second phase of the canal construction, 1832–1845 (Author)

The next length opened was to Withington on 26th February 1844 to great celebrations;

The completion of the Canal has been for some time regarded as an object of great importance to this city and county, and the circumstance of the work having been finished up to Withington about four miles only from Hereford, was therefore hailed with much satisfaction. A more suitable occasion indeed for paying a just tribute of respect and approval to Mr. Stephen Ballard, the talented engineer, for the manner in which he has conducted the work throughout the entire line, could scarcely have been chosen, and he was accordingly invited to a public dinner, which was given at the Hotel on Monday last....

In pursuance of the previous arrangement a procession of five boats left Ledbury at nine o'clock the same morning, the first containing a band of music, the next the committee and friends ; one with goods belonging to Messrs. Bunning and Gibson ; one the property of Messrs. Crowley, ditto; and one salt from Droitwich. These boats were all decorated with union-jacks, flags, &c and had a very pleasing appearance. About twenty-seven other boats freighted with coal, &c. followed in the course of the day. The view from the wharf at Withington along the line of the Canal to the lock, was extremely picturesque, and the whole scene was peculiarly animating. On the wharf itself from fifty to sixty labourers were employed, and the whole preparations and arrangements were completed in a very short space of time.

No accident of any consequence occurred, the only circumstance of this kind being that of a horse led by a respectable inhabitant of this city getting into the canal, where he was soon released without sustaining damage.

Hereford Journal: February 28th 1844

The great and the good of Herefordshire then repaired to the Green Dragon Hotel in Hereford for a night of dining and extravagantly optimistic speeches.

The euphoria surrounding the opening to Withington was to be short-lived. In the space of only a few months the tide turned. Ballard's diary takes on a depressing tone:

> Received a letter from the Manager of the Gloucester Bank saying we could not overdraw our account any more. I wrote and told him we must for paying the men tomorrow, this gave me great annoyance and I spent a most miserable day...
>
> Paid men at tunnel today and discharged a great many...
>
> In extremely low spirits, vexed at the affairs of the Canal. The trade does not go on well, we have very little work to do to complete and the Railways are coming in from the north and south...Railways are everywhere and no funds to complete our little work without personal security.
>
> *Ballard, Stephen: Diary entries for March 28th – March 31st 1845*

Perhaps it was in this state of affairs which led him to ask the Committee if he could be released:

> Mr. S. Ballard having requested the opinion of the Committee as to the possibility of their dispensing with his services at present, and the Committee having taken the state of the works into their Consideration
>
> Resolved – that in the present unfinished state of the Canal the Committee do not consider that they would be justified in consenting to release Mr. Ballard unless a sufficient portion of his time could still be occasionally guaranteed for the General Superintendence of the Business of the Canal Company, and such is the opinion of the Committee as to Mr. Ballard's integrity of purpose on all occasions that they readily leave to himself the determination of this question."
>
> *Ballard, Stephen: Diary entries for April 21st 1845*

This itself is an indication of the highest esteem in which Stephen Ballard was held, though there is no evidence that he was called upon to return to Herefordshire after his departure.

Work continued, including the 440 yards tunnel beneath Aylestone Hill which was completed at remarkable speed, the final 63 yards being completed in a fortnight. On May 22nd 1845 Stephen Ballard and his brother Philip lifted the stop planks to fill the basin. In contrast to the celebrations at Withington, the event passed off un-witnessed and almost unnoticed. The Hereford Times carried a brief and complimentary report of the engineering feat, but was only mildly enthusiastic as to its future benefits:

"The Canal. Hereford and Gloucester Canal is now opened to this city, which will soon have a remarkably spacious basin, warehouses, &c, at Monkmoor. On Wednesday water was admitted through the tunnel at Holmer, a stupendous work, which we have before described, and boats can now come on to the city. It must have been a source of high satisfaction to Mr. Stephen Ballard, the engineer, to witness the triumph of this important undertaking before leaving for Lincolnshire, where some important works have been confided to his superintendence. The cuttings on the Hereford side of the tunnel are really tremendous, reminding us of some of the awful railway excavations in Derbyshire, and the whole work is one of great skill and extent. The tunnel has a towing-path, and like the aqueduct overt the river Lugg exhibits all the evidences of durability for future ages. The advantage of the canal in the conveyance of Staffordshire coal and all kinds of produce, will soon be experienced by the inhabitants of this city and the surrounding neighbourhood."

Hereford Journal Nov 28th 1845

Figure 5: The Middle of the three Hereford basins, coloured from a contemporary etching.
(Hereford City Library)

Ledbury to Hereford

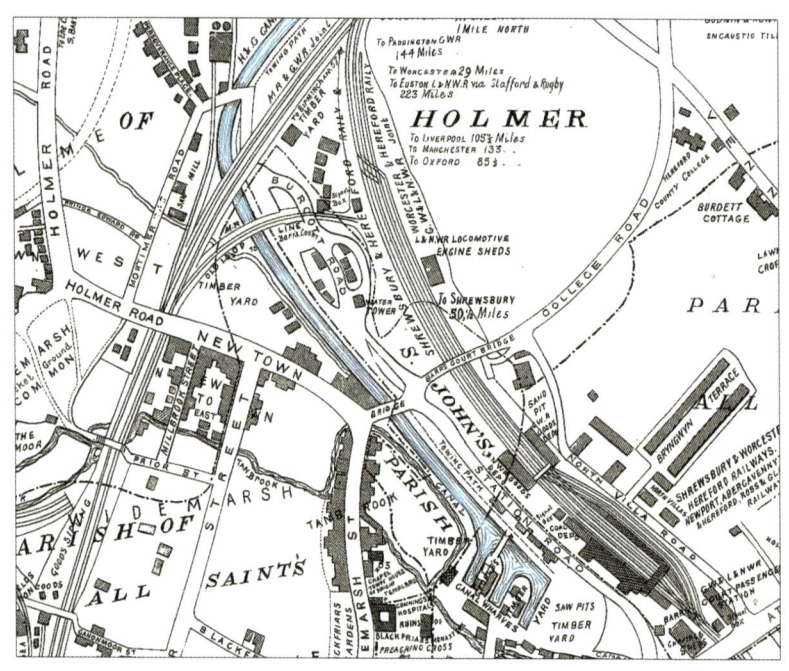

Figure 6: Part of a map of Hereford showing the canal and terminal basins dated 1885, two years after the traffic ceased on this part of the canal.

The canal was complete. Ballard had given his all, probably knowing that the inevitable coming of the railways would surely make the whole project nonviable. He left Herefordshire the same day to begin work on the Middle Level Drain in the fens. The words of his diary are now well enough known, but worth repeating in full here;

> Canal opened to Hereford. This morning had the satisfaction of seeing the water turned into the basin at Hereford. It was contrived that I should see it before I started for London.
>
> "I was greatly affected at leaving Withington, it was a fine morning and the country looked beautiful. I could not refrain from shedding tears. Near 18 years I have been employed on the canal and my spirits dropped when the hour arrived for my leaving it. Went from Gloucester to London by GWR. Bad headache.
>
> *Ballard, Stephen: Diary entry for May 22nd 1845*

Before we allow Stephen Ballard to leave our story, though he will reappear very briefly later, a little more must be said about this exceptional man.

40

A Remarkable Man

When planning the first edition of this book I decided that I would limit my mention of Stephen Ballard to his involvement with the canal and say little about the man himself. But no one reading his diaries and other writings can fail to realise that there was far more to Stephen Ballard than just a skilled engineer. I therefore added another chapter which I have expanded in this edition.

The best account of his life to date can be found in Pamela Hurle's delightful 'interpretation' entitled "One of Nature's Gentlemen" to which I would refer any reader who would know more about Stephen Ballard. I am grateful to Mrs. Hurle for her willingness to allow me to share some of her extensive knowledge and enthusiasm with my readers.

We are fortunate to have the benefit of Stephen Ballard's diaries which he kept for much of his working life. Now held in the Hereford Records Office, these were written in Odell's Shorthand, one of five different systems introduced in 1832 but became obsolete for many years ago. These were partly transcribed by his grandson, another Stephen, and recently, more fully with reference to other writings by Ballard, by the late Geoff Warren, a member of the Canal Trust for many years.

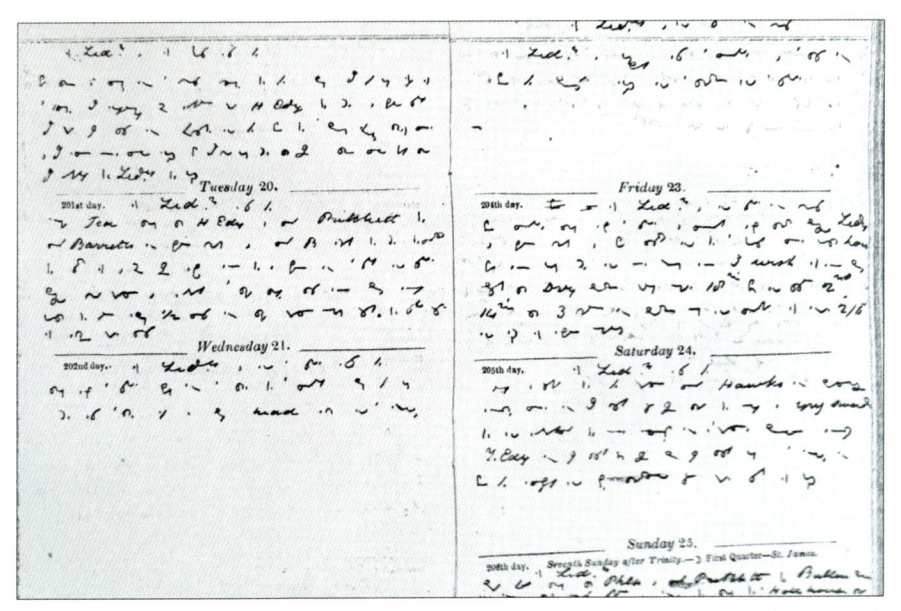

Figure 1: Stephen Ballard's diary entry for the week of July 19th 1841 (Sue Warren)

A Remarkable Man

Stephen Ballard was born in 1804, significantly, in a house standing on Malvern Link Common. While his indifferent education ill-prepared him for life as an engineer, from his early childhood he developed a great love of the countryside surrounding his home which led him to teach himself botany. Stephen's father was an attorney, but the family was not at all well off, a situation exacerbated by his father's heavy drinking and an unsuccessful libel action.

Charlotte, his mother, whom he greatly adored, taught him honesty, the virtue of hard work and thrift, values which he never lost throughout his long life. She also supplemented the family income by taking in lodgers, some of whom were surprisingly well connected. One such was the Dowager Duchess of Donegal, Barbara Chichester, who had been widowed at the age of 31 in 1799.

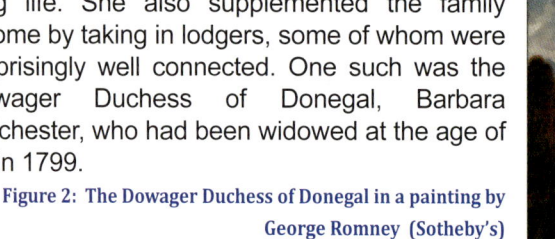

Figure 2: The Dowager Duchess of Donegal in a painting by George Romney (Sotheby's)

Through her influence, Stephen, at 18 years of age, secured a position at Lea and Kennedy's nurseries which were part of the Chiswick House estate, in Hammersmith.

Figure 3: Chiswick House, where Stephen Ballard received his first training in horticulture (A coloured engraving from the Yale Center for British Art)

42

A Remarkable Man

After only a year Stephen left London to work at Hewell Grange near Tardebigge, Worcestershire, on the Earl of Plymouth's estate. The beautiful landscaped gardens here had been laid out by William Shenstone and remodelled by Capability Brown in 1768. The young Stephen Ballard was keen to learn the skills of managing a large country estate.

Figure 4: Hewell Grange in a coloured lithograph (British Library)

Before long, the Dowager Duchess again used her influence, this time securing him a position at Kew Gardens. But Stephen could see no future for himself, and perhaps for a family in due course, simply as a gardener. He wanted to set up in business himself but had no means of raising the necessary capital, so turned down the post at Kew and decided to look for a totally different profession.

In 1825 he became apprenticed to a well-established Cheltenham builder, Henry Lucy, a position into which he threw himself with great enthusiasm. But Lucy's business failed two years later, and through the influence of John Biddulph, at the age of 23 Ballard found himself Clerk to the Hereford and Gloucester Canal Company.

Knowing little of civil engineering, he was sent by the Company to see some of the great engineering works currently in progress – both railways and canals. With a mind like a sponge, he soaked up concepts and solutions to problems and by the time he returned home he was ready to put his ideas into practice. Soon he was working with the young Robert Stephenson planning a seven-mile feeder from Canon Frome Mill to Ledbury in order to provide a reliable water supply to the canal. Because of a lack of funds the Company was unable to build it but rewarded Ballard with £20 in recognition of his 'zeal and activity'

He headed up north visiting the canals in Shropshire and around Manchester, straying into Wales to examine Telford's new bridges crossing the Menai Strait and the River Conwy. He visited Chat Moss to see how George Stephenson had 'floated' his railway line across the moss, a huge swamp of mossy peat.

After completing the Hereford and Gloucester Canal to Hereford in 1845 he departed immediately to the fens to begin work with Messrs. Walker and Burges, "*The great nursery of civil engineers in England*", on the new Main Drain from the Great Ouse to the junction with the sixteen-foot river at Upwell.

It was at Cambridge Railway Station in 1847 that Ballard is said to have accidentally bumped into Thomas Brassey, already established as the leading railway contractor in Britain, having constructed about a third of all the lines so far built. From this unlikely beginning a mutual respect grew between the two men, born within a year of each other, and they worked together on a number of major projects in Britain, Europe and India including the line between Bedford and London and one of the most difficult sections of the Great Northern Railway through the fens.

One of Ballard's last major projects, also with Brassey, was the building of the Worcester and Hereford Railway, which opened in stages from 1859. This involved two tunnels under the Malvern Hills. The tunnels, at Colwall (1,567 yards) and Ledbury (1,323 yards) were particularly difficult due to the hardness of the rock. The route also required the crossing of the Leaden Valley on a 30-arch brick viaduct built by Stephen's brother Robert, using five million bricks made on the site from the clay dug out for the pier foundations.

Figure 5: Ledbury Railway Viaduct running 62 feet above the Leadon Valley (Mr M.E Ivison)

A Remarkable Man

The opening ceremony in 1861 was slightly delayed because the lady who was to lay the last brick, a Mrs Richards, missed her train from Hereford and arrived half an hour late!

While working on the canal Ballard had been constantly frustrated in dealing with the owners of land through which it was to pass. Now the boot was on the other foot as the railway line ran though part of Ballard's own The Winnings estate.

When the railway company agent opened negotiations with him he is said to have simply replied "take it at your own price". He believed the railway would bring a prosperity to the area which far outweighed any loss the landowners might incur.

Figure 6: Stephen Ballard (Lyn Ballard)

From quite an early age Stephen Ballard had shown some talent as an inventor. His ideas included a design for building timber lock gates without the use of any iron, and a "scorcher" which was pulled by a horse and threw flames onto the ground to burn off wheat stubble.

One of his most notable inventions was his ice-breaking boat, demonstrated in Ledbury in 1838 and for his account of which he was later awarded the Telford Medal by the Institution of Civil Engineers, the highest prize awarded by the Institution for a paper or series of papers.

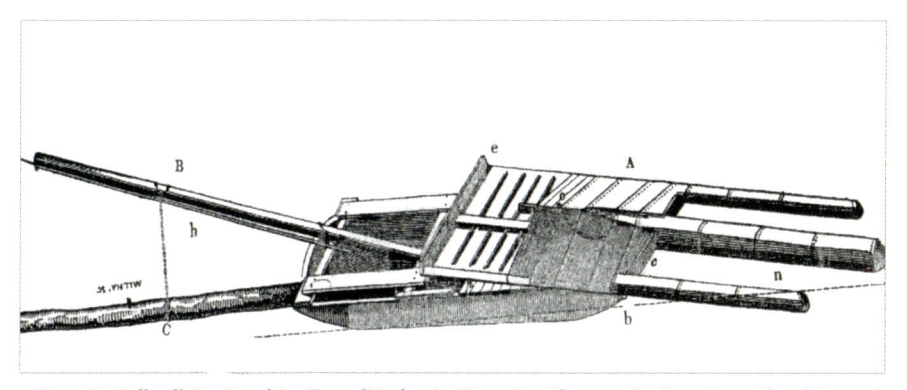

Figure 7: Ballard's Ice-Breaking Boat (Mechanics Magazine, Museum, Register, Journal and Gazette)

> Long pieces of timber, cased with Iron, were fixed on the front of the boat, these timbers project before the boat, and form an Inclined plane, sloping upwards from the under edge of the ice to near the middle of the boat. By these means, when the boat is drawn forwards, the ice is forced upwards Instead of downwards, as is the usual way of breaking; and It is found the Ice breaks remarkably easy when thus lifted from the water. The boat, with its apparatus, was drawn along the canal by two horses at a brisk pace, and the ice, which was in some places upwards of four Inches thick, was ploughed up with great facility... It is calculated that one horse will do as much work with a machine of this kind as four in the common way.
>
> *(Mechanics Magazine, Museum, Register, Journal and Gazette)*

His interest in railways continued right up until his death, only a few weeks before which he published the second edition of a pamphlet which argued the case for a cheaper form of railway which could be built to serve rural areas. In the post-Beeching railway era, his ideas make interesting reading:

> A line suitable for a rural district should be made for about £4,000 a mile. The gradients may be 1 in 25 and the curves of 4-chain radius; thus allowing the line for the most part, to be made on the surface of the ground, with very little cutting or earthwork. The speed of trains should be restricted to 15 miles an hour, thereby vastly reducing the wear and tear of the permanent way and rolling stock. Light tank engines would be sufficient; and as in most cases the line would be short, only one engine at a time would be on the line, thus avoiding collision and expenses in signalling. Light tank engines running only at moderate speed would allow of frequent stoppings for the accommodation of the district. The conductor of the train should act as general station-master, receive fares, and manage the traffic of the line; thus saving a great deal of the expense attending stations.
>
> *Ballard, Stephen: "Cheap Railways for Rural Districts", 1890 p.7*

Though he became prosperous in middle to later life he always had a concern for the poor. There are many references in his diary like the following, not, I am sure, to boast about his generosity because the sums are, to him, quite trivial. He just relates what happened. In 1839 he tells us :

> "Went from Bristol to Gloucester by coach. Walked to Newent and then coach to Ledbury. There was a poor woman from Stratford in the coach and as she seemed in distress I told the coachman I would pay her fare from Gloucester."
>
> *Ballard, Stephen: Diary entry for December 16th 1839*

In 1840 he writes:

> Payday. Holland has been at work for a month but on measuring up there is nothing to come to him. He was in great trouble and offered me his watch if I would lend him £4. I would not take it but advanced him the money which I expect he will never pay.
>
> *Ballard, Stephen: Diary entry for July 11th 1840*

Ballard tantalisingly mentions an incident while the deep Ashperton Tunnel was under construction, about which I would love to know more details: *"Boy fell down shaft No. 4, 60 feet deep. Was with him until 1am."* Of course, the boy shouldn't have been playing anywhere near the construction works, but this was 1841 and I like to think Stephen saw something of himself in that lad, having spent his childhood exploring the Link Common and no doubt getting into all sorts of mischief himself

His diaries also tell us something about his opinions. He frequently mentions his frustration with unreasonable landowners and he has little sympathy for members of the legal profession.

> "Went to Worcester to try and get Hill to reduce his bill (£34) of costs for defending father in the libel action. He would only take off £4. Said he had charged as low as he possibly could, which I do not believe. He is like other lawyers, will say and do anything for money."
>
> *Ballard, Stephen: Diary entry for June 13th 1839*

His view of race meetings was similarly uncompromising;

> Ledbury races. Did not go near them as I considered that they ought not to be supported on account of the fighting and drunkenness which is encouraged there.
>
> *Ballard, Stephen: Diary entry for August 24th 1838*

He uses identical wording to describe the Hereford races! While still a bachelor, his views of women are interesting too;

> Philip and his wife went to Ledbury to see the American Riders perform. I do think that the principal object of a woman's life is pleasure, they are always seeking it and most of them think of nothing else.
>
> *Ballard, Stephen: Diary entry for August 3rd 1842*

A Remarkable Man

Perhaps this had changed by 1854 when Stephen married Maria Bird, the daughter of a farmer on whose land he had worked on the construction of the Great Northern Railway. They must have seemed an unlikely couple. At 25, Maria was half his age and, unlike her husband, totally devoid of any sense of humour.

Their marriage was to last 36 happy years and brought eight children into the world, all of whom survived into adulthood. In 1855 the couple moved into the new centrally-heated home Ballard designed on his Colwall estate. At the back of the house, adjacent to the kitchen was a large porch with seating for those who might come begging for a bowl of soup. And come they did, for in a letter to the Daily News he writes;

> Over 5800 basins of soup a year are given to the hungry poor at my back door. The plan adopted is this: a large stock pot is constantly in use on the kitchen fire range. Into this pot scraps of meat, bones, gravies and other edible scraps of provisions are put and then thoroughly stewed; thickening of rice, split peas with salt and pepper are added and the result is a savoury and nutritious soup....A very considerable amount of extra work is entailed on the cook, not only in making the soup but mainly in giving it away to the hungry applicants. This extra labour the cook cheerfully submits to, working people generally have a kind and charitable feeling for those who are in want.
>
> *The Daily News, February 1886 quoted in Hurle, Pamela: Stephen Ballard 1804-1890 "One of Nature's Gentlemen" p89*

His generosity towards the poor was not universally admired. In response to a remarkably modern argument, he goes on;

> Some objections are made to this method of helping the starving poor on account of the danger of encouraging regular tramps that never will work. Occasionally such idle impostors may be supplied but only a small proportion of the whole. Most of those supplied are working men, out of work and are worthy objects of charity. The fear of erring by encouraging an occasional idle tramp I think should not prevent the practice of saving food from waste now the very great proportion travelling are without doubt working men.
>
> *(Ibid)*

Though he was not, it seems, quite as enthusiastic a church-goer as Maria and his children, his views are remarkably resonant with John Wesley's words written in his Journal 133 years before: *"So wickedly, devilishly false is that common objection, 'They are poor only because they are idle'"*.

Unlike Wesley, Ballard was a confirmed teetotaller and was opposed to capital punishment for any crime, even in 1836, the year of the last hangings in England for offences such as arson, burglary and rape, but still 32 years before the last public execution was carried out and 133 before it was abolished altogether.

There is no evidence that he changed his view after his older brother Philip, was murdered in 1887 during a burglary at his home in Hereford while his own daughter Ada was staying with him. James Jones and Alfie Scandrett were hanged in Hereford gaol the following year for the offence.

While he designed a number of public buildings in the area, perhaps his greatest legacy to the nation is found in the Malvern Hills themselves. The Hills had been part of a Royal Forest since the days of William the Conqueror but under Charles I this had become common land controlled by the Lord of the Manor. The law relating to commons is extremely complex and obscure and over the years this had enabled significant areas of the Hills to be taken into private ownership. Many poor people depended upon their common rights to graze sheep, pigs and cattle and to gather wood, nuts and berries. During the 17th century protests among the poor became frequent, characterised by anonymous poems written at the time;

They hang the man and flog the woman, Who steals the goose from off the common, Yet let the greater villain loose, That steals the common from the goose.

The law locks up the man or woman Who steals the goose from off the common And geese will still a common lack Till they go and steal it back.

By the middle of the 19th century this had become a serious issue, not only for the poor, but for the more affluent who saw their rights of access to the hills being steadily eroded and the condition of the land itself deteriorating. The main local culprit, in the eyes of many, including Stephen Ballard, was Lady Emily Foley whom he saw as stealing land from the poor. Lady Foley was no great admirer of Stephen Ballard either. She refused to travel by train through his Colwall Tunnel, preferring to travel by horse-drawn carriage to Great Malvern Station where she had a private waiting room, now Lady Foley's Tea Room.

The Malvern Hills Preservation Association had been set up in 1876 with the intention of managing the Hills for public recreation but did not want to interfere with what it described as "vested rights". The Association failed to understand those very rights protected the interests of landowners and commoners with grazing and other Common Rights but these conflicted with the recreational facilities the Association wanted to secure.

A Remarkable Man

In 1881 Ballard and a local academic Robert Raper, who was to become the first Chairman of the Malvern Hills Conservators, led a successful legal challenge to protect an area of the common at Barnard's Green.

Through letters to local newspapers and arranging and addressing public meetings Stephen Ballard and a small group of prominent local men was largely responsible for the Malvern Hills Act of 1884 which established the Malvern Hills Conservators, preserving the rights of the Commoners and giving the right of public access to the hills which we enjoy today. His last piece of engineering work was the design of the magnificent Jubilee Drive, running across the western flank of the Malvern Hills, opened in 1889 to celebrate Queen Victoria's 50th jubilee,

He died in 1890 at the age of 86 and was buried on his Colwall estate over his tunnel. His obituary in the Journal of Institute of Civil Engineers reveals much about the man, as well as the engineer;

> Perhaps no employer was ever regarded with more real respect and affection by his workmen... They felt that their master was a friend in whom they could place implicit trust.
> *Journal of Institute of Civil Engineers, 1891*

Figure 8: Stephen Ballard's greatest legacy - the right of us all to enjoy the Malvern Hills. Just a small number of the many people on a fundraising walk over the Hills organised by St. Richard's Hospice, Worcester in 2022 (Imaginary Friends Photography)

Uncertain Times

The lack of interest shown by the people of Hereford to the arrival of the canal seems to have continued once the canal was fully operational. The canal had cost far more than Ballard had ever imagined and initially there was insufficient toll income to pay even the interest on the Company's loans. The threat of the railway hung over the whole enterprise with various schemes proposed, including one using the line of the canal itself, but they came to nothing.

The fears raised by the Gentlemen of Hereford in 1791 regarding the "serious Inconveniences and Mischiefs" which would result from the building of the canal were realised soon after it was completed. In 1849 the following letter appeared in the Hereford Times:

Sir, —Through the medium of your paper, I beg leave to call the attention of the police to the practice of bathing in the canal near the bridge at Widemarsh and close to the public road, where there are many persons continually passing. At about four o'clock on the afternoon of Friday last, as I passing near the spot, my attention was attracted by seeing a crowd of persons on the bridge, and on looking to see what "puppet show" attracted their attention, I saw a naked fellow nearly grown to man's estate on the bank of the canal near to the bridge, exposing himself in the most indecent manner. Some music was being played in the street near the wharf, and this shameless fellow mounted some boards at a very short distance from the road and commenced dancing to the tune, a gentleman of the city, with a lady, being passing over the bridge at the time, the former cried shame that such a scene should be allowed. The fellow, having amused himself by dancing as long as he pleased, returned in a state of nudity, not by water, but along the towing path to the wharf near the Commercial-road, where I suspect he had left his clothes. I thought the best accompaniment to his dance would have been the tune of a policeman's cane applied vigorously to his naked body; he might have been then made to "dance without a fiddle." Really, Sir, it is disgraceful that such things should be allowed so near a public thoroughfare, and I trust the police will give "a sharp look out!" Hereford, June 27th, 1849. OBSERVATOR

Hereford Times: June 27th 1849

Uncertain Times

The problem of people bathing in the canal was not new. Back in 1843 when a new section of the canal in Ledbury had opened the Hereford Times had commented:

> BATHING IN THE CANAL: Notwithstanding the notices which are posted on the several bridges near the town, to caution parties against bathing in the Canal, the practice, we are sorry to say, still continues. It is scarcely possible to conceive a more pleasant walk than that along the banks of the new portion of the Canal; and it seems a particularly favourite one the females, especially on the Sabbath evening. But many are obliged to forego the pleasure on account of its being converted into a public bathing station; the practice of bathing there not being merely resorted to by boys, but by fellows who are old enough to know better. We trust that the constables will sometimes take a walk by the canal side on a Sunday evening, and bring to justice offenders of this description.
>
> *Hereford Times Saturday June 24th 1843*

Traffic gradually increased and the Company was able to meet its interest payments by 1847, but the promises of the early promoters of the canal were never realised. Even before the canal was open the proprietors had looked for ways to get rid of it. Initial interest was shown by the snappily titled Herefordshire, Gloucestershire, South Wales and Worcester Railway and by the Welsh Midland Railway, but like other attempts over the next few years, nothing actually happened.

In 1853 the railway line between Hereford and Shrewsbury opened, 130 tons of rail having been delivered by canal to Widemarsh two years previously. The Newport, Abergavenny & Hereford Railway opened only a month later. In 1855 the Great Western broad-gauge line from Gloucester which ran through Tintern and Ross was opened to Hereford, thereby killing off most of the remaining barge traffic on the River Wye.

During the early 1850s the various companies vying to link Hereford to Worcester were too busy fighting among themselves to take any interest in the struggling canal. The hopes that this line would utilise the route of the canal failed to be realised when a more direct route ignoring it altogether was approved in 1853, though the line wasn't opened fully until 1861.

The Company struggled on. The Post Office Directory of 1856 gives only one coal agent at Hereford's Barr's Court Wharf – E. Pinkerton and one coal dealer, E. George. However, Ledbury Wharf was full of coal dealers – B. Bill, J. Bill, Mrs A Davies, W. Pitt, T. Rees and E. Webb. There were others in Bye Street and Bridge Street. J. Racster was a coal agent at Withington. Perhaps it is significant that two other coal merchants in Hereford are given as being "above Eign" suggesting that the Wye was still carrying significant amount of coal into Hereford. Pickford and Co., Danks, Venn and Sanders and Henry Mounsell and Co. were the main carriers working *'by canal etc. to London and all parts'*.

By 1848 the order restricting the use of the canal to the hours of daylight had clearly been lifted and as traffic increased it was necessary to control the passage of boats through the long Oxenhall Tunnel which was too narrow for two boats to pass each other. Boats travelling towards Gloucester we allowed to enter the tunnel between the hours of 3 am – 6am, 9 am – 12 noon, 3pm – 12pm alternating with the timings for boats bound for Hereford but it seems unlikely that there was a tunnel-keeper on hand to ensure these timings were observed.

The use of the canal at night was an exception to normal practice, though gas lighting was used on the busy Birmingham Canal Navigations for Netherton Tunnel and the Farmers Bridge lock flights.

At an inquest recently held, touching the death of Thomas Lanslett, of Ledbury, in the county of Hereford, labourer, who was drowned during the night of 2526 January 1848, in the narrow tunnel on the Hereford and Gloucester Canal leading from Dymock towards Newent, and known as the "Oxenhall Tunnel", when helping John Beard to "leg" through the tunnel one of the boats belonging to Mr. Holloway of Withington, near Hereford, common carrier. The Jury with their verdict included the following presentment to the Coroner: ...Also that some change is required on the part of some of the carriers on the said canal as to the requirements from their servants, in regard to the number of hours of continuous work by night and day, and the constant of the entire Sabbath.

Hereford Journal, February 9m 1848

53

Uncertain Times

In 1948 the Hereford Journal was concerned about the safety standards on the canal in general and the use of it at night and on Sundays in particular.

There was another drowning in 1850, and again the Hereford Journal expressed its disquiet:

> It seems rather strange that theft should be so many fatal accidents in the narrow Boat Canal between Gloucester and Ledbury while there are so few in the Ship Canal from that port to Sharpness Point. This fact would induce an opinion that there must be something radically wrong in the navigation or management, perhaps both, of the former. Some are inclined to attribute it to the construction, others to the working of it by day and by night, Sundays and week days, depriving the men of their necessary rest and sleep; While others suggest the use of improper cattle and tackle; it may be that all combine in a measure to occasion them.
> *Hereford Journal: February 20th 1850*

The comparison between the Hereford and Gloucester canal and the Ship Canal (the Gloucester and Sharpness Canal) was most unfair. The Ship Canal, apart from the junction with the Severn, had no locks nor tunnels and the swing bridges were all operated by the Canal Company. The Hereford and Gloucester Canal required boatmen to operate its 22 locks, some of which were unusually deep and the three tunnels were narrow, one without a towpath. There were far more opportunities for accidents to occur than on the Ship Canal. There is little to suggest that there were more accidents on the Hereford and Gloucester Canal than other narrow canals.

In May 1851 a remarkable case was brought before the Newent magistrates after a complaint that two boats had obstructed the navigation for some 12 hours. A boat owned by Mr. Collingbourne of Gloucester had entered the tunnel but suffered a delay during its passage. Sometime afterwards a boat owned by Mr Smith of the Kerry Arms, Hereford, apparently assuming the tunnel was clear, entered the tunnel through the other portal.

After meeting in the middle of the tunnel neither boat was prepared to give way and other boats entered the tunnel. In a rather confused account, the Hereford Journal reported that it was a full 24 hours before the tunnel was eventually cleared.

A week later it was obliged to publish a correction:

> Stopping the Navigation on the Canal. - In consequence of our Reporter having misunderstood his informant, we represented in last week's paper, that, in the case heard at Newent, several boats remained within the Tunnel, at Oxenhall, from 12 o'clock one night till 12 o'clock the following day-a period of 12 hours; whereas, the truth is, they remained in their dark, dreary, and subterraneous abode, from 12 o'clock on the Thursday night till 10 o'clock on the following Sunday morning—a period of 58 hours! Those who are acquainted with the Tunnel at Oxenhall will think it almost incredible that a number of human beings should, because neither party would give way to the other, choose to remain so long in such a situation. There is no towing-path through the tunnel; but the men, as have before said, lie on their backs, propel the boats through with their feet. Water is continually falling from the low roof, and, altogether, a more damp and dismal place cannot be imagined.
>
> *Hereford Times. May 31st 1851*

Two years later a similar incident occurred:

> Warning to Boatmen—John Beard, a boatman, was summoned by Mr. P. Ballard, of Hereford, clerk to the Herefordshire and Gloucestershire canal company, for obstructing a boat in the tunnel of the Herefordshire and Gloucestershire canal. The defendant had been navigating his boat from Gloucester to Ledbury, and at the time when he entered the tunnel at the end, he ought to have been out at the other end towards Ledbury. In consequence of his being so late he met a boat navigated by Samuel Boon, and there being room for only one boat to pass it a time, they stopped each other. Neither party would go back; and there they lay for nine hours until other boats came up from Gloucester, entered the tunnel, and forced Boon, the complainant, out of the tunnel the way he went in... The case was proved by Samuel Boon Richard and Good, the lock keeper, and Beard fined £4 ten shillings an hour being the full penalty.
>
> *Hereford Journal, August 13th*

The report of Beard's fine of four pounds ten *an hour* could hardly have been correct, amounting to over £40 if we count nine hours. This would be more than

Uncertain Times

a boatman could earn by a journey from Hereford to Staffordshire and back. More often, the canal was obstructed by shortages of water after prolonged dry weather. 18 boats were stranded at Canon Frome in August 1842 and freight loads were restricted in 1872. The long pound between Rudford and Over was particularly at risk because of the very deep river lock at Over.

The cold winters of the last three decades of the nineteenth century also caused problems. In 1871 the entire canal was frozen for several weeks and had to be cleared by an ice-boat hauled by six horses.

In 1854 the Company did a deal with the newly opened Newport, Abergavenny and Hereford Railway to carry coal from Hereford to Newent at a discounted rate. Presumably the boats carrying this coal would meet those bringing coal from the Forest of Dean coming the other way!

Rescue, if it can be called that, came through the influence of the extraordinary William Philip Price. Dr. Price, owner of Tibberton Court, notable philanthropist and twice MP for Gloucester, was Chairman of the Canal Committee but also held influential positions connected with a number of other canals and railways. His business partner, Richard Potter had similar connections. He had been a member of the Great Western Board until 1856 and in 1860 became a Director of the West Midland Railway. When the West Midland and Great Western amalgamated in 1863 he returned to the GWR board and served as Chairman until 1865 when he was replaced by Sir Daniel Gooch.

Between them, on January 17th 1862 Price and Potter managed to broker an agreement with the Great Western and West Midland Railway Companies to lease the canal and enable a railway line from Ledbury to Gloucester to be constructed on the route of the canal. The Memorandum of Agreement began as follows:

> The Canal to be bought by the Railway Companies for a perpetual rent charge of £5,000 per annum to commence from the 1st day of January 1862 payable half-yearly on the 15th day of July and the 15th day of January. The Canal and Railway Companies parties hereto bind themselves either one or both as may be decided upon to apply for an Act of Parliament to confirm this purchase and to convert the whole or a part of the Canal into a Railway in the same session of Parliament that a Bill shall be applied for to amalgamate the Great Western, and West Midland Railway Companies.
>
> *Memorandum of agreement between Herefordshire and Gloucestershire Canal Company and the Great Western and West Midland Railway Companies, January 17th 1862*

Uncertain Times

The canal was to be run by a Joint Committee of members of the three companies until such time as a new Act of Parliament could be obtained transferring ownership. After it had absorbed the West Midland, the Great Western was in no hurry to obtain the new Act or to convert the canal to the railway and the Joint Committee had to remind the Great Western of the Agreement several times. Matters were not formalised until the Great Western Railway (Canal Vesting) Act was passed in 1870. The official wording which appears in the London Gazette runs to several pages and deals with seven new interconnecting railway lines. In relation to the section from Ledbury to Dymock we read the following:

> "To authorize the Company to stop up and discontinue the navigation of that portion of the Hereford and Gloucester Canal, now vested in the Great Western Railway Company, which lies between Dymock and Ledbury; and to appropriate and utilize for title purposes of the intended railways, all or any part of the said canal between the places aforesaid, freed and discharged from all duties, liabilities, and responsibilities connected with that part of the said canal, and to enter into and give effect to agreements between the Company and the Great Western Railway Company for the sale and purchase of that part of the said canal, and to authorize the Great Western Railway Company to sell the same and to substitute stock, either with or without a preference or priority, of that Company for the canal rent charge of £5,000 per annum, now payable under the Great Western Railway (Hereford and Gloucester Canal Vesting) Act, 1870, to the Company of Proprietors of the Herefordshire and Gloucestershire Canal Navigation."
>
> *London Gazette, November 26th 1872*

Similar provisions relate to the section of the Canal between Newent and Gloucester. Much of the line of the canal between Dymock and Newent, including the long tunnel at Oxenhall, was avoided by the railway, which explains why this part remains in water to the present day.

Despite now having the power to close half of the canal, the Great Western was in no hurry to begin work on their new railway line. It continued to operate the canal for a further nine years before issuing a closure notice.

A glimpse of the canal in Ledbury was given in the Ledbury Reporter in 1955 when it published some of the childhood memories of Mr. Ernest Bill, then aged 85. Ernest was a boy of 11 when the canal closed and he remembers helping to unload the very last cargo of timber to be carried along the canal. His father owned one of the three main canal carrying companies at the time in Ledbury.

Uncertain Times

Figure 1: Over Lock : A painting from the school of Edward Smith (from a private collection)

Uncertain Times

The principal cargoes, he recalled were corn, timber, coal, salt and 'various delicacies'. Cider and perry were loaded onto boats at the Old Wharf on the Ross Road having been stored in the Old Cyder warehouse.

Figure 2: Ledbury Old Wharf and Cyder Warehouse (from a private collection)

Ernest Bill also recalls the lighter fly boats "which used to ferry groceries from Gloucester to Hereford stopping at many villages on the way. He also remembered the Ledbury boatmen:

"The canal provided employment for many men. For not only were there bargees, but crane men, lock men, loaders and a skilled band of "puddlers," who kept the waterway in order, repairing leaks and trimming banks.

"In those days, the coal loaded into a barge was measured by displacement of water (the barge having been previously weighed), and Mr. Bill remembers an old story of a local barge owner who sent his newest barge to the official weighers fitted with a heavy oak bottom.

"Having been measured it was returned to Ledbury, where he craftily removed the oak bottom and fitted a nice light deal one With this dodge be regularly 'gained' extra coal from the unsuspecting merchants."

Ledbury Reporter 1955

Uncertain Times

Near Ledbury gas works a spectacular collision occurred in 1873.

> Accident on the Canal. - An accident occurred on the Hereford and Gloucester Canal, near the town on Friday evening, by which traffic will be stopped for a few weeks. A man in the employ Of Messrs. Danks, the canal carriers, was towing a boat, and when near the lock at the Ledbury gasworks it was driven with such force against the gates that they burst open. Some of the masonry disturbed and one of the gates was torn away and carried a considerable distance down the canal. The man in charge of the boat, who at the time was on the landing of the gates, about to open them, was thrown into the lock between the boat and the wall, and miraculously escaped unhurt. In consequence of the accident the water burst forth with such force that the new gasworks were for a time considerable flooded.
>
> *Ross Gazette, September 4th 1873*

This was by no means the first incident of its kind. In December 1851 a whole series of cases had been brought before the magistrates in Hereford.

> ANOTHER LOCK-DAMAGING CASE. Two men named Perrins and Symonds, in charge of a boat the property of a person named Perks, were charged with having wilfully damaged one of the lock gates on the Hereford and Gloucester Canal. Symonds did not appear, having, it was stated, absconded on Saturday morning. The case was, however, gone into against Perrins; but it appearing from the evidence given that he did all he possibly could to avert injury done to the lock-gates, by holding the strap until his strength failed, with the view of preventing the concussion that afterwards took place between the gates, it was agreed to abandon the case against him and proceed against Symonds, who had, contrary to the directions of Perrins, raised the rudder of the boat before it had passed the upper gates, - Symonds was fined £3 and expenses, and in default of payment, to be imprisoned for six weeks.
>
> James Harper, a boatman, was then charged with having, through neglect, damaged one of the lock-gate. on the said Company's property. The defendant admitted the offence, and was fined £2 and 7/- expenses, Mr. Ballard saying that in that instance he would recommend a further mitigation the Company.
>
> *Hereford Journal, December 10th 1851*

Uncertain Times

Philip Ballard reported two incidents to the Committee in 1869, one concerning another Danks's boat in a collision at Oxenhall. Quite what the steerer was doing at the time is a mystery, but the response is typical of a kindly Ballard.

> "I have to report that James Bayliss has been fined by the Magistrates at Ledbury £2.0.0 and expenses for ramming his boat against Staplow swing bridge, but it subsequently turned out he was insane, and is now in a Lunatic Asylum, the fines and expenses have not been paid. I am also sorry to report that a steerer of Messrs Danks's boats has been fined £2.0.0 and expenses for allowing his boat to strike the upper gates of Oxenhall No.2 Lock, but as it appears he was unavoidably absent from his boat at the time I returned him one pound of the fine".
>
> *Company Minute Books September 30th 1869*

By the 1870s trade on the Hereford and Gloucester Canal had declined to a trickle and the accounts we read of the state of the canal come from a then unlikely source – tourist traffic!

In 1873 a party consisting of Mr. Farrant and three companions undertook a major holiday round trip from Oxford via Warwick, the Severn to Gloucester, Hereford, and the River Wye to Chepstow. Putting their boat on the roof of a train they crossed the Severn and by the Kennet and Avon canal and the Thames they returned to Oxford. All this in three weeks and in a rowing boat, occasionally assisted by a sail! Their trip on the Hereford and Gloucester Canal took two days and it seems to have rained most of the time. They found the canal very narrow and full of weed but thought the entrance to Oxenhall was very pretty. Passing through the tunnel they took advantage of the acoustics with some merry singing. They met little traffic, except just outside Hereford when their mooring lines seem to have become entangled with the tow line of a passing boat.

Much more detail about the canal is given in the log of another holiday on the canal two years later.

Mr. Howard Williams and his companions visited the canal in another rowing boat in 1875 and his account provides a rare detailed account of the state of the canal.

Figure 3: Howard Williams' Rowing boat sketched by one of the crew (Waterways World)

They too seemed to experience a lot of rain, but their first problem was to find the way in:

> "We saw on the map that a branch of the river about a mile above Gloucester led direct to Over, where we had to get into the Hereford & Gloucester Canal and we, of course, intended going along this branch, but some men that I spoke to told me that there were several weirs in it and no locks, so that we could not go that way but would have to follow the main stream, go through Gloucester and round Alney Island to Over. These men either knew nothing at all about it or else were most abominable liars, for the lock-keeper at Over afterwards told us that the branch was quite clear and was the usual route for barges.
>
> "We very soon after this approached Gloucester ... The water here was very dirty and the streets that ran alongside the river equally so. We were very glad to get out of it and round the bend through a lock to Over. Here we went into a deep lock which leads to the canal. Fred and I climbed up the wall and went into the lock house while the other three took the boat through. I asked for our pass and the man made it out for me and wanted to charge 15/- but fortunately I had a letter with me which I had received in London from the Canal Company stating that the charge would be 10/-. This I triumphantly produced. So the man was done out of his expected bonus."

The ambitious crew had hoped to reach Dymock that night but had not bargained for the state of the canal. While they found the countryside as beautiful as they had ever seen anywhere, reeds covered the water just leaving a few feet for a narrow boat to pass. From the towpath their boat was hidden by reeds six to eight feet high which made towing difficult to say the least. They then encountered the double, or staircase, locks at Malswick:

> "It was an immense thing with about 30 feet fall and a pair of gates in the middle. None of us had ever come across such an affair as this before and we had no idea how to manage it. There was not a soul to be seen so we could get no information on the subject. We took the boat in, shut the rear gates and let down the sluices, then opened the middle gates and let in the water at the top sluices, but by some extraordinary means the water, as soon as it came in, rushed out again through some invisible exit and as there was a ledge across the middle of the lock we could not get sufficient in to float over.

Uncertain Times

> We experimented here for over half an hour. At last we made a tremendous effort and having let the water in with a rush, by means of pulling with boat hooks and tugging at the sides, we managed to get over the ledge and float in the upper half of the lock. Our difficulty then was over, for we had only to shut the middle gates, when the upper half soon filled and we easily went through. This was the only lock of its kind that we came across during our tour and to this day I have no idea how it is worked."

The total rise of these locks is actually nearer 17 feet than 30 but in a rowing boat must still have felt somewhat threatening. With rain on and off adding to their discomfort they eventually reached Newent where clearly tourists were a novelty.

> "We landed at a wharf close beside the bridge on which a large crowd soon assembled to see us disembark. We locked all the moveables up in a barn which the proprietor of the wharf kindly placed at our disposal and gave the boat in charge of some bargees who had their craft moored alongside. A mile beyond Newent there is a tunnel nearly two miles long, which we had to go through. We made enquiries of the bargees about the hours of going through and they told us that craft going in the direction of Hereford would have to go through between the hours of 6 and 9 and 12 and 3, both fore and after noon"

Clearly there was no longer night working on the canal and the next morning, after negotiating four more locks, they tackled Oxenhall Tunnel but they found it less pretty than had Mr. Farrant two years before;

> The tunnel had not a very inviting aspect. It was very small and narrow and looked more like a sewer than anything else. It was so small that two craft going in opposite directions could not pass each other. That is the reason why there were specified times for going through. The bargees lie on their backs on the top of their barge and push along the roof with their hands and feet. We lit our lamp and entered at 7.25. George and Clarke sat in the stern, Tom and Fred pushed along on either side with boat hooks and I knelt in the bow with the lamp. Very soon after we had got in the tunnel made a turn and we could see neither one end nor the other and were in complete darkness, with the exception of the glimmer from the lantern, which only made the darkness visible. It was a melancholy sort of place, not calculated to put one in the liveliest spirits, so I started a song, which revived us all, and we sang part-songs and choruses all the way through. It sounded very well, too, echoing and reverberating along the tunnel.

Uncertain Times

Sadly, though clearly a tradition in the 1870s, the singing of part songs and choruses is no longer common practice while negotiating canal tunnels. After dodging a series of waterfalls from the roof they reached the end in only 35 minutes, having been misinformed as to the actual length of the tunnel. and began to enjoy the countryside again, despite the rain.

The canal was clearly in a bad condition being once again obstructed by reeds. During their whole trip there is no mention of any other boats on the move.

> Outside the tunnel the banks were again very beautiful, similar to the first 5 miles of the canal. Tom and George attempted to scull here, but the canal was so narrow and the water so covered with rushes that they soon gave up and Tom took the towline whilst Clarke went ahead and opened the gates and locks. Clarke was followed for some distance by a drove of little pigs.
>
> There must have been something very peculiar about him to attract pigs in the way he did. Once before at Heyford a similar thing happened. It was a fearfully dull and miserable day, a damp mist falling and occasionally rain. We passed through 7 locks before we reached Ledbury, where we landed, leaving the boat in charge of a lockman. It was raining at the time, so we walked up the town in full wet-weather costume, mackintoshes, leggings and sou'westers, and carrying the cans in our hands. The people rushed out to the shop doors to look at us and no doubt we did present a very curious appearance."

After shopping in Ledbury, but unable to purchase any milk, they returned to their boat.

> We stopped about an hour in Ledbury then went back to the lock where we had left our boat and which we found surrounded by a swarm of little children. We sculled on for about half a mile, hoping they would disperse, but about half a dozen of the dirty little enthusiasts were evidently bent on seeing us eat our lunch, for they would not go away, notwithstanding the most awful threats. We pulled up under a bridge for lunch and as they still hovered about, George made a rush after them. He caught one and held him over the water, threatening to drop him in unless he made off with his companions.

The Canal and River Trust do not regard this as an appropriate means of dealing with the unwanted attentions of children today.

Uncertain Times

The rest of the journey to Hereford passed with little incident, though the towpath through Ashperton tunnel was virtually impassable due to six inches of mud and the crew were obliged to let Fred, who had been towing, join them in the boat which they then pushed through with boat hooks.

Alfred Watkins, the noted antiquarian and discoverer of ley lines (if they actually exist) lived in Herefordshire all of his life. Writing in the early 1930's he recalls the canal just before it closed:

> Early in 1881, hearing it was about to be closed (the embankment at the Ledbury Station end of the new Ledbury-Dymock railway having already started), I persuaded another young boating spark, (Ted George, whose father had founded a timber business at the Canal Wharf at Hereford), to come with me on a two days' final water-trip by canoe along the whole length to Gloucester. A very jolly trip it was, chasing down ducks who flew and flapped in terror at the strange invaders, diving through tunnels with a small boat's lamp, to give light, carefully balanced on the bow, and shouting songs to keep our spirits up in the case of that long weird tunnel (1¼ miles) at Oxenhall, where we could not see the other end and were paddling into the blackness of night, with the water washing the walls on both sides, for in this one the tow-path went over the top of the hill, and the canal-men had to leg their barges through by pushing with their feet against the roof.
>
> Watkins, Alfred: Herefordshire in his own words and photographs. Logaston Press

When the Great Western actually got around to building their new line, construction began at Ledbury enabling materials to be transported by canal from the Severn. Due warning was given in June 1881, giving just 28 days for all "Barges, Boats and other craft to be removed accordingly".

The Ledbury Free Press reported the draining of the canal in 1881 and solved the mystery of the whereabouts of the missing head of the town pump:

> The past week will be memorable in the annals of Ledbury consequent upon the closing of the canal between this town and Gloucester. The operation of the letting off of water from the Hereford road bridge commenced on Monday last, and the canal is now cleared as far as the leather-mill lock. Among the many secrets laid bare by the removal of the water, not the least noteworthy is the recovery of the head (of the) town pump, the loss of which was recorded in these columns a few years ago.
>
> Ledbury Free Press July 12 1881

65

By 1883 all traffic had, at least officially, ceased. The Hereford to Ledbury section, now isolated from the rest of the canal network carried some local traffic for a year or two but for the next hundred years little would be heard of this canal. For the Company though, financially at least, these were the Golden Years. Until the eventual nationalisation of the Great Western in 1945 the proprietors received their annual rent of £5,000. The Company had no boats, no salaries and no maintenance – in fact, no costs at all. The good Dr. Price had struck an excellent deal.

HEREFORDSHIRE AND GLOUCESTERSHIRE CANAL.

IN THE MATTER OF THE NEWENT RAILWAY ACT, 1873,

AND

IN THE MATTER OF THE ROSS & LEDBURY RAILWAY ACT, 1873.

TAKE NOTICE, that in pursuance of the powers in that behalf contained in the Newent Railway Act, 1873, and the Ross and Ledbury Railway Act, 1873, it is intended on and after the 30th day of June, 1881,

TO STOP UP AND CLOSE

so much and such part of the CANAL known as the Herefordshire and Gloucestershire Canal as is situate BETWEEN the Worcester and Hereford Railway at LEDBURY in the county of Hereford and the River Severn in the City of GLOUCESTER, and that all rights of way or navigation and other rights and privileges, if any, along, upon or over such part of the said Canal, with the banks and towing path, will as from the said 30th day of June cease and determine accordingly.

AND FURTHER TAKE NOTICE, that all persons who will be affected by the closing of the said portion of the Canal are required, on or before the said 30th day of June, to remove their Barges, Boats, and other Craft accordingly.

Dated this 2nd day of June, 1881.

BY ORDER.

Figure 5: Notice of Closure issued in June 1881 (Janet Moult)

Accidents and Crimes

In telling the story of the canal we have referred to some of the accidents and misdemeanours which occurred during the operation of the canal itself. But, like other canals, there were both accidents and crimes which involved members of the public.

We have space for only a brief selection of such incidents and will allow the newspapers to tell much of the stories – though it has been necessary to edit many of them as often quite trivial incidents were reported at great length. I am grateful to the www.ledburyhistory.uk website for much of the material for this chapter. It has saved no end of trawling through the British Newspaper Archive! Like other canals, safety arrangements surrounding the canal were minimal and there are numerous accounts of people falling in. Mostly these were not serious incidents, but many involved children:

> FORTUNATE ESCAPE FROM DROWNING. On Friday last, two girls, each about 10 or 11 years of age, one of them carrying an infant of about 15 months old in her arms, attempted to cross a plank placed across an arm of the canal, made for the reception of canal boats, at the Bye street wharf, when the three were precipitated into the water.
> Fortunately for them, some persons who were present on the wharf went to their assistance, and rescued them from what would otherwise soon have proved their grave.
> *Hereford Times, November 1st 1845*

> NARROW ESCAPE FROM DROWNING: On Thursday se'nnight, a boy, between eleven and twelve years of age, fell into the canal, at the mouth of one of the locks, near Bye street wharf. He could swim a little, but, instead of attempting to reach the land, swam into the lock, and made several ineffectual attempts to climb up the lock door.
> We wonder much that many more accidents do not happen in the neighbourhood of Bye street; for there, at any time of the day, may be seen children, who can but just walk, tottering along, at the water's edge, without any attendant able to protect them from danger. Such shameful neglect in parents is highly reprehensible.
> *Hereford Times August 1845*

Accidents and Crimes

Less fortunate was Robert Smith who drowned at Withington Wharf in 1857:

> CHURCH WITHINGTON —DEATH BY DROWNING. A few days ago, as Mr. Greenaway, a boat owner on the Hereford and Gloucester Canal, was loading his vessel with apples at Withington-wharf, his nephew, a lad named Robert Smith, attempted to walk along a plank stretched from the boat-side to the canal bank. Somehow he slipped from the plank, and disappeared under the boat, which was moved off, and the boy was with some difficulty rescued from the water. He was most carefully tended by his aunt and uncle, and had the benefit of Mr. C. Lingen's surgical skill, but the poor little fellow lingered until the following day, and then died.
>
> *Hereford Times 28 November 1857*

It wasn't only children who drowned:

> On Wednesday, the body of an old man, named Vale, found in the paddle hole of the lock leading out of the basin of the Herefordshire and Gloucestershire Canal at Ledbury. The unfortunate man left his home the Saturday previous, and was returning in the evening, when, it is supposed, his foot slipped in passing over the plank at the top of the lock gates. The party, in search of him were attracted to the spot, where he was found from the circumstances of his dog barking having been heard howling in the neighbourhood on the Saturday evening and also on the following days.
>
> *Hereford Times May 10th 1834*

Only one of the locks had a handrail and foot board – an unthinkable omission today. Almost certainly nine-inch planks were often laid across the canal to allow people to cross. At least one lock-keeper was drowned while working his lock.

Another child death was the subject of an inquest in 1851 concerning the daughter of Joseph Holloway, a boatman of Hereford. His name appears in a number of newspaper reports between 1851 and 1860.

> INQUEST LEDBURY: CHILD DROWNED On Wednesday last, at the Bridge Inn Ledbury, on the body of Sarah Holloway, a child about six years old. It appeared that the unfortunate little girl was the daughter of Joseph Holloway, of the Burcott Row Hereford, an owner of boats trading on the Herefordshire and Gloucestershire Canal, who has three

Accidents and Crimes

other children besides the deceased. One of his little girls was staying in Ledbury and had been ill with the measles. The father took his two sons and the deceased to Ledbury to see their sister. The children were left in a boat on the canal, and it is supposed that the deceased, coming on deck, fell overboard, but no one saw her drowned. Her body was found by her afflicted father and a man named George Baldwin, in about five feet of water. The poor child was quite dead when discovered.

Deceased, who was a remarkably quick and intelligent child, attended Miss Venn's school, where she was only on Friday last, and her aptitude for learning caused her to be a great favourite with her instructress. She was only taken from Hereford on Sunday last, and early on Monday morning was, alas, a corpse. Her parents are deeply afflicted. The verdict of the jury was: Found Drowned

Hereford Times June 28th 1851, the body of an old man, named Vale, found in the paddle hole of the lock leading out of the basin of the Herefordshire and Gloucestershire Canal at Ledbury. The unfortunate man left his home the Saturday previous, and was returning in the evening, when, it is supposed, his foot slipped in passing over the plank at the top of the lock gates. The party, in search of him were attracted to the spot, where he was found from the circumstances of his dog barking having been heard howling in the neighbourhood on the Saturday evening and also on the following days.

Hereford Times May 10th 1834

Only 10 days later we read:

DREADFUL ACCIDENT. It is this week our painful duty to record a shocking accident which befel Mr Joseph Holloway, of Woodyard Cottage, near Burcott ROW in this city. The unfortunate sufferer is an owner of boats, with which he trades on the Herefordshire and Gloucestershire canal. We hear that, on Sunday last, he was at Ledbury, and was making use of a crane for the purpose of loading or unloading, when some heavy substance fell from the top of the crane, and alighting upon his ankle smashed it to a dreadful degree. Surgical assistance immediately had recourse to, but amputation found to be necessary, and the poor man's leg was amputated below the calf. It must be in the recollection of our readers that, a few weeks ago, Mr Holloway had an interesting little girl drowned in the canal at Ledbury.

This second sad event making the proverb correct that "misfortunes seldom come singly".

Hereford Times August 9th 1851

Accidents and Crimes

A quite bizarre story concerning a drowning at Oxenhall in 1852 was reported in the Derby Times. Whether this drowning took place in the canal or in the pond near the locks, a remnant of the watercourses powering Ellbridge Mill, isn't clear, but the story is too remarkable to omit.

> ALLEGED FULFILMENT OF A DREAM. A most singular instance of the fulfilment of a dream has transpired at Newent, Gloucestershire. An inquest was held at that place, on Monday, before Mr. Lovegrove, one of Coroners of Gloucestershire on the body of a man named Mark Lane who had been found drowned under most remarkable circumstances. The evidence of the deceased's brother was to the following effect: He was informed on Friday night that his brother Mark was missing; he immediately replied, "Then he is drowned for I dreamt last night that he was drowned and that I was up to my arm-pits in water endeavouring to get him out. " That very same night the man dreamt again that his brother was drowned near the locks at Oxenhall, and there he saw a trout by him. Next morning he went to Oxenhall another brother and there he saw a trout in the water He felt convinced that the body of his brother was near, and, in fact the body was found near in spot. The deceased, it appeared, was addicted to drinking and on attempting to pass home along the road, which was flooded he was carried away by the stream and drowned. The verdict of the jury was "Found drowned."
>
> *Derby Mercury December 8th 1852*

In July 1853 a very serious but localised flash flood occurred at Dymock.

> The village of Dymock, Gloucestershire as many of our readers are probably aware, lies in a valley, and is passed several hundred yards to the north side by the Hereford and Gloucester Canal on a lofty embankment, rising above the level Of the village something like a hundred feet. At three o'clock on Friday morning the thunder rolled heavily and forked lightening occasionally lit up the surrounding country. Scarcely a breath Of air stirring. Suddenly, as we were informed, an intensely black cloud came across the sky, and discharged an immense volume of water over the village, the canal and the country lying on the north side of the stream...the level of the canal was simultaneously raised and the water topping the banks swept over the adjoining country.
> ..
>
> *Hereford Journal 13 July 1853*

Accidents and Crimes

It is hard to imagine an embankment 100 feet above Dymock – it was actually more like 10 feet, but the press seldom lets exaggeration get in the way of a good story.

A number of boats were arriving at the north portal of Oxenhall Tunnel, the Hereford side. One of these was owned by Messrs Gibson:

> Gibson's men had nearly arrived at its mouth on the Hereford side, when they found themselves suddenly lifted by the rising water, so much so as to render it necessary to cut down the short mast to which the "lines" were attached. A sudden rise in the of the water under such circumstances must have given rise to apprehensions in the minds of the men of the most unpleasant character. At this juncture, it appears - and it was most fortunate for the men that it was so - the bank burst and gave the water free vent, at the same time shooting the boat out at the mouth of the tunnel.
>
> *Ibid*

The prospect of being in the narrow, claustrophobic tunnel with the water rising so quickly hardly bears thinking about, but the boat suddenly being propelled backwards away from the tunnel cannot have been pleasant either - and there were other boats behind Gibson's:

> Immediately in the rear was a boat belonging to a man name Hodgetts, laden with corn for Mr. George Bateman. When this boat and that of Messrs Gibson got clear Of the tunnel they became wedged together, and stuck in the side of the embankment — an unlucky incident under normal circumstances, but in this case most fortunate, for both must have inevitably been carried down the embankment into the village. A mass of water was flowing from the land over the mouth of the tunnel, and in a brief period the soil thus washed by the water actually formed an embankment in the bed of the canal into which the bow of Mr Holloway's boat was driven, and this became a fixture!
>
> *Ibid*

We have met Mr Hodgetts in the previous chapter in connection with his delinquent horse and can only assume that this animal was not involved here. Mr Holloway seems to be particularly accident prone.

There were also problems at the other end of the tunnel, but, remarkably, it appears that all concerned in this incident escaped unscathed.

Accidents and Crimes

> Mr George's boat was in the tunnel when the immense body of water met it, but to the side of the tunnel. Soon afterward it was drawn back again by the receding waters, caused by the bursting of the banks at Dymock. It now lies laden with lath, slate and timber in the middle of the tunnel 3/4 of a mile from either side.
>
> Mr Goode, the lock-keeper at Oxenhall, was greatly surprised and alarmed to see a vast and irresistible body of water flowing along the canal towards Newent, especially as no rain had fallen in that neighbourhood. Shortly afterwards Goode was as much surprised as had previously been to see the body of water receding, nor could he account for such a phenomenon until he heard the news that the canal bank had burst on the other side of the tunnel. The water was up to the third stair of his house, although it lay so high.
>
> *Ibid*

In Victorian times boatmen were often regarded in much the same light as vagrants and gypsies. They were here today and gone tomorrow and their children were largely uneducated and were presumed to live in squalid conditions. On land, a room with less the 900 cubic feet of air was considered unsuitable for habitation, but on a narrow boat complete families lived in space with less than a third of that. By many, the boatmen, and even their women, were seen as hard drinkers, sometimes with unpleasant consequences for those who crossed their path. They were often suspected of poaching or pilfering, helping themselves to chickens or eggs where these were near the towpath.

In his account of working life on the canals, Narrow Boat, L.T.C. Rolt, who knew these people well, albeit towards the end of regular freight carrying, paints a quite different picture, one of honest men and women working long, hard hours for little reward. Perhaps the truth lies somewhere in between but press reports of boatmen falling foul of the law are quite rare. But certainly there was some crime on and around the towpath. The reporter for the Hereford Times clearly enjoyed telling this story:

> ASSAULT; On Thursday last Jane Holder, alias Miss Trowsers, a precious gem of Bye Street summoned Caroline Gale, a very lovely flower of the same locality, for assaulting her in the street. Miss Caroline was ordered, by magistrates, to pay 8s 6d, which included expenses.
> MISS CAROLINE GALE AGAIN: Miss Caroline, who was on Thursday last the defendant, appeared this day (Tuesday), as a complainant, and preferred a charge against Mrs Charlotte Hope of Bye Street of pushing

Accidents and Crimes

her and a male companion into the Herefordshire and Gloucestershire Canal.. Mrs Hope denied the charge, and brought forward several witnesses to prove her innocence. From the evidence of the parties, it would appear that Miss Caroline, and her companion, were both in such a state of intoxication, that they walked direct into the canal without any person touching them, and then fancied she had been pushed pushed in by the party who was nearest to her. Miss Caroline was equally unfortunate as a complainant, as when she was a defendant, for she was ordered to pay the expenses, which amounted to 8s 6d, but the lady declared she sooner revisit her old quarters than submit to such a thing. She was allowed a short time to consider the matter and decide which of the two steps she would take.

Hereford Times July 30th 1842

The magistrates took the case of William Parson's much more seriously:

Wm Parsons was charged with stealing at Ledbury one hundred weight and a half of coals, the property of William Restell. Mr Cooke called the prosecutor, who stated that on the 2nd of January he had a boat at the Ledbury and there were some coals in it; he left the coal in charge of the prisoner, afterwards he missed some of the coal, and prisoner on being asked about it, said he had burned it. Wm James said that he saw Parsons at the Ledbury Wharf on the 2nd of January, and there bought of him some coal which he stated to be his own, and for which he gave him 6d and a gallon of cider. Prisoner in his defence said that Mr Restell allowed him to sell coal, which the latter positively denied. Verdict. Guilty. Four months imprisonment, first and last fortnights to be solitary.

Hereford Journal March 21st 1838

A somewhat amusing story, also about coal, appeared in the Hereford Times in 1848. It seems that two coal merchants at Ledbury Wharf, Mr. Godwin and Mrs. Webb were used to helping each other out when their stocks were getting low:

LEDBURY: CHARGE OF STEALING COAL. Anne Davies alias, Webb, aged 36, who can neither read or write, was placed in the dock, charged with having, on the 7th and 8th days Of December last, stolen a quantity of coal, the property of Mr William Godwin.
Mr Skinner conducted the prosecution and Mr Cooke defended the prisoner. Mr William Shead was the first witness called, who deposed

Accidents and Crimes

> that he is a police-superintendent for the Ledbury district, and knows Mr Godwin, the prosecutor, and his stack of coal on the Ledbury wharf; he also knows the prisoner at the bar and her stack of coals; in consequence of information which he received, he went to the wharf and saw Mrs. Webb (the prisoner) lock the gate of her coal-wharf ; another person was passing near the wharf; in two minutes after the other person had passed witness the defendant pass from her own yard to Mr Godwin's stack of coal and take a lump there from; witness then went up to her, took her into custody, and told her she had a lump of Mr Godwin's coal; to which accusation prisoner replied "Lor, Mr Shead" the prisoner then told witness she merely took a lump to it, and said "God bless you, don't say anything about it".
>
> *Hereford Times January 8th 1848*

Under cross-examination Mr Gilbert admitted that he actually owed Mrs Webb well over a ton of coal which he had borrowed from her. Mr. Cook, acting for Mrs Webb gave the following very reasonable explanation:

> ... in consequence of the prosecutor owing her coal, and she being required to send a sample of coal to a customer, and her own stack being low, she, thinking the prosecutor would return what he owed her, took a lump from his stock to send a sample to her customer.
>
> *Ibid.*

Hardly surprisingly, the jury found Mrs Webb not guilty of the charge.

The Company also suffered from vandalism, especially, it seems, in Hereford between Burcott Row and Aylestone Tunnel:

> Thomas Radbourn, a man dressed as a boatman, appeared to answer the charge preferred against him at the instance Of the Hereford and Gloucester Canal Company by their Clerk, Mr. Ballard, for damaging the bridge over the canal near Burcott Row, known as the old Racecourse bridge. Mr. Pritchard conducted the Case, and called a little boy named James Jenkins who deposed to having seen the defendant on Thursday last push a stone off the parapet-wall of the bridge in question and afterwards throw it into the canal.
>
> Mr. Ballard proved that he had examined the bridge and found a great quantity of the stones on both sides removed; depredations and damage to the property of the Company along the line of the canal had of late

Accidents and Crimes

> been very frequent, especially within the liberties of the City Of Hereford, where injury had been done to the amount of at least 15s.
>
> The defendant's excuse was that he accidentally knocked off the stone, which was very loose, with his elbow and a companion came forward to corroborate him but his almost unintelligible story only tended to support the charge.
>
> Hereford Journal September 5th 1849

The cost of the damage inflicted by Radbourn was estimated at six shillings, which he had to pay, but this probably reduced the fine that might otherwise have been given to £1.7s.10d. The 'Mr. Ballard' referred to here was Philip Ballard, who was now acting as Company Clerk, the uncle of Stephen Ballard.

The Company may have thought he had got off lightly as it published a reminder to any would-be vandals informing them that:

> ... every such offender shall be guilty of a felony, and if convicted, shall be liable at the discretion of the Court to be transported across the seas for life, or for any term not less than seven years, or to be imprisoned for any term not exceeding four years: also, to be once, twice or thrice whipped in addition, if the Court shall think it fit.
>
> *Ibid*

There were, of course far more serious crimes that Mrs Webb's theft of a lump of coal or occasional acts of vandalism. One such involved Joseph Holloway the Hereford boatman who, as we have recorded, lost both his daughter and his leg at Ledbury and was caught up in the Dymock flood of 1853.

> SHOCKING RUFFIANISM On Sunday a boatman, maddened with stolen wine, committed a series of atrocities whilst upon the Hereford and Gloucester Canal at Oxenhall, near to Newent, in this county. It seems that a boat proprietor named Butler was walking along the canal when he met by some children, who ran to him screaming and entreating him to save their mother, who was "being murdered by their father. Butler hastened to the spot, and found a woman, nearly under, struggling in the canal. He succeeded in getting her out, and then her husband, a boatman named Holloway, commenced an attack upon him, during which, rushing upon him with an open knife, he inflicted a gash in his throat three inches long and stabbed him in four other places in the neck and face.

Accidents and Crimes

> Mrs Butler, coming up to her husband's aid, Holloway hurled her head foremost in the canal. Another woman, who had taken some part in the affair, was also thrown in by the infuriated fellow, who again set upon Butler (who, though profusely bleeding from his wounds, was attempting to draw his wife out of the water) and precipitated him in al An aged man now came up, but he had no sooner commenced to remonstrate than he too was hurled in by Holloway. In all no fewer than five persons were in imminent danger of drowning at the hands of this drink-maddened boatman. All were, however, got out safely.
>
> It has been ascertained that Holloway, was apprehended on Monday, had been drinking freely of some wine that was being conveyed in casks on board another boat then lying in the canal; and that dragging his wife from her bed, he had thrown her, undressed, into the canal twice before Butler came up.
>
> *Bristol Dally post, July 5th 1860*

Holloway, with his wooden leg, drenched wife and terrified children on board then set off towards Hereford. It later transpired that most of the people involved in the story were also involved with the theft of the wine.

> SERIOUS CHARGE OF STABBING Joseph Holloway (46), a boatman, with a wooden leg, was charged on an indictment with having, on the 1st of July, stabbed and wounded Charles Butler, with intent to do grievous bodily harm at Oxenhall. This case arose out of the wine robbery tried on Monday, and the prosecutor was one of the prisoners who were convicted of the robbery. It appears that the prisoner, prosecutor and several other men and had drunk very freely of the stolen wine.
>
> *Hereford Times 7th 1860*

An extremely serious case was heard at the Hereford Assizes in 1857 when a single woman, Harriet Rudge, was indicted for the murder of her child James, who was found drowned in the canal near Bosbury. She was seen in a lane leading from Bosbury to Ledbury, carrying the child, and soon afterwards was seen returning without it. On April 1st the body of a child was found in the canal, near that road, in a state of decomposition. It is to the jury's credit that, in an age when a working-class single mother might not expect much sympathy from a jury of 12 land-owning gentlemen, it delivered a not guilty verdict on the grounds that the identification of the body was not satisfactory.

Accidents and Crimes

Not all crimes were solved, as this harrowing account of an Inquest in 1867 shows:

> Mr. J. U. Fawke, agent for the carrying firm of Danks and Sanders, deposed to the finding of a parcel near the bridge in Mr. Barnes meadow. A man who was in the boat with him cut the string confining the parcel, which smelt so badly that they threw it over the bridge into the meadow. Wither waiting to see what the parcel contained. They also saw a second parcel, but did not interfere with it. George Brookes, a little boy 12 years of age, deposed to getting the second bundle out of the canal.
> John Fleetwood, police-constable, found the body of one of the children in Mr. Barnes's meadow ; it was brought to the Bridge Inn; and while he was engaged talking to Mr. Griffin, the surgeon, he was informed of the finding of the second body. Had made diligent enquiry, but was unable to attach suspicion to anyone.
>
> *Hereford Journal August 31st 1867*

Finally, mention must be made of a crime committed on October 19th 1887, four years after the last traffic on the canal. The victim was the elderly Philip Ballard aged 87, the brother of Stephen Ballard. Philip has worked for some years as the Company Clerk after Stephen had left Herefordshire to work on in the fens.

In the early hours of October 19th 1887 two 23-year-old men, Alfred Scandrett and James Jones broke into the home of Philip Ballard at The Knoll, Tupsley on the outskirt of Hereford. It is likely that only burglary was intended, but in the course of ransacking the house they were disturbed by Philip and Scandrett attacked him with an axe, dealing him two violent blows before running from the house. The household had been awakened by the noise and Stephen Ballard's daughter, Ada, who was staying at The Knoll, discovered her badly injured uncle. Philip's injuries were such that he died four days later.

Scandrett and Jones were later arrested and confessed to the murder. Although Scandrett had actually struck the blows, under principle of Common Purpose both men were hanged at Hereford Gaol in March 1888.

Dark Ages

Once the canal had been closed and most of the line between Ledbury and Gloucester obliterated, the canal rapidly passed from public awareness. Between Hereford and Ledbury much of the canal was infilled and embankments levelled and ploughed up, but considerable lengths remained holding water, especially either side of Ashperton Tunnel. During the Second World War it was proposed that Aylestone Tunnel might be used as an air-raid shelter, but, still being full of water, this was not pursued.

One by one the simple milestones which marked the route disappeared, only one is now known to be complete with its plate remaining in its original position. At least one other stone remains insitu with its plate removed for safe keeping, but possibly others survive in the more remote and inaccessible parts of the towpath. Two others have been moved by their owners to protect them.

Figure 1: The sole known remaining intact original milepost
(Mike Potts)

Road improvements required the culverting of some of the old stone canal bridges, but a surprising number survived. It is likely that much of the stonework from locks and bridges was taken away to be given a new life elsewhere. It certainly disappeared.

Very few photographic records survive from these years, but some have been preserved to give us a glimpse of the canal as it faded from memory.

The canal crossed two rivers of some consequence, the Lugg and the Frome, both on substantial aqueducts.

There are varying opinions as to when the low stone-arched Lugg Aqueduct was demolished. A widespread belief that it was blown up by the Home Guard during World War II is contradicted by recollections that it was still standing in the 1950's. The Lugg Drainage Board is unable to confirm either view. It was almost certainly demolished to reduce flooding and it is said that when the Lugg is running very low the base of the piers are visible under the water, but in recent years I have been unable to confirm this.

Dark Ages

Figure 2: The River Lugg aqueduct (Mike Clarke Collection)

The Frome Aqueduct has also disappeared and photographs exist which almost certainly show it being demolished, though the exact date for this demolition too is still something of a mystery.

Figure 3: River Frome Aqueduct (Mike Potts)

Dark Ages

Figure 4: The Frome Aqueduct under demolition (Mike Clarke Collection)

Gradually almost all signs of the canal in Hereford disappeared. The basins were not filled in until the 1950's and there are local people who still remember canoeing in them. The canal offices were demolished in 1983, just before the Herefordshire and Gloucestershire Canal Society was formed and which might have campaigned to save it.

Figure 5: The former Canal Offices in Hereford, demolished in 1983

Dark Ages

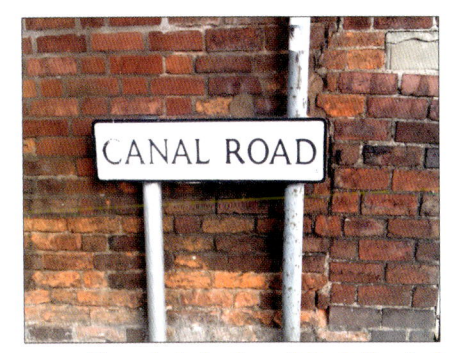

Figure 6: An ironic road sign in Hereford (Author)

Once these had gone, only Widemarsh Street bridge and the sign in Canal Road bore visible evidence of the existence of the canal.

Ironically, when the canal was open, what is now called Canal Road was part of the present Monkmoor Street. The original Canal Road led to the wharves from the corner of Station Road near its junction with Commercial Road.

In Gloucestershire most of the canal line was quickly obliterated by the building of the Ledbury–Gloucester railway.

The exception to this was the section beginning south of Dymock, which avoided the Oxenhall tunnel to rejoin the canal line just north of Newent. Here the canal survived largely intact, much of it in water.

Only two bridges survived from the first phase of the canal built from 1793 to 1798, Cold Harbour Bridge, just south of Oxenhall Tunnel and Boyce Court Bridge to the north of it.

Figure 7: The South Portal of Oxenhall Tunnel from an old postcard (Mike Potts)

On the Ledbury to Hereford section of the canal more bridges survived, several road bridges still carrying traffic today. Other bridges were replaced by culverts or demolished completely.

All three tunnels survived, though the portals of the Oxenhall Tunnel suffered badly. The northern portal was intact until the 1930's but by the 1960's had almost entirely disappeared. The two shorter tunnels survived almost undamaged, a tribute to Ballard's engineering work.

81

Dark Ages

Figure 8: Part of the lined section at the South end of Oxenhall Tunnel (Private collection)

Figure 9: An unlined section of Oxenhall Tunnel looking towards the South portal (Private collection)

Dark Ages

Figure 10: Another view of the tunnel in the unlined section. Although 'officially' only nine feet wide, this wider section may be due to a roof fall. It might also be a point in the tunnel where attempts at mining coal were made during the construction of the tunnel (Private Collection)

Dark Ages

A few glimpses of the canal from the early years of the last century are to be found in old post cards, most of which feature the section of the canal between Dymock and Ledbury. Very few postcards of the canal in Herefordshire have survived, if indeed, many were ever produced.

Figure 11: An old photograph of the canal bridge at Boyce Court, one of only two which were not obliterated by the building of the railway (Tim Ward)

Figure 12: Skating on the canal at Newent (Mike Potts)

A significant number of buildings associated with the canal have survived to the present day, mostly restored quite independently of the canal, and these will be described in Chapter 17. They include a fine cluster around the wharf at Withington, although the wharf itself is represented only by a few coping stones along its edge. The wharf house itself has survived, though somewhat altered, and until relatively recently the words "William Bird - Wharfinger" could clearly be made out on the wall.

Figure 13: The Wharfinger's house at Withington. The name William Bird can just be made out painted on the brickwork (Mike Potts)

It was this fading inscription which inspired the name of the Herefordshire and Gloucestershire Canal Society's magazine.

Another wharf building at Withington once bore the word SALT on its end wall, just visible when photographed in the 1960s.

Figure 14: The Salt Warehouse at Withington (Mike Potts)

Dark Ages

A similar inscription could be seen on the side of a wharf building at Canon Frome Wharf where an old warehouse also survived together with the support of the wharf crane. This rare example of a crane column is presumably not the original at Canon Frome, for in July 1854 Stephen Ballard reported that the crane at Canon Frome Wharf needed replacing as it was "in a decayed and dangerous state."

Figure 15: The sadly overgrown and decaying remains of the stone warehouse at Canon Frome Wharf (Mike Potts)

Figure 16: The crane column at Canon Frome Wharf (Mike Potts)

There is nothing now visible of the various wharves which served the canal in Ledbury, indeed there is some mystery as to exactly where some of them were. It has long been thought that the Old Wharf was on the Newent side of the Ross Road, on the site later occupied by the Countrywide store and now by an assortment of retail outlets. A long building believed to be navvies' accommodation dating from the time of the building of the canal was demolished to make way for the developments on this site.

Figure 17: Navvies' accommodation in Ledbury on the site south of the Ross Road, now demolished (Mike Potts)

Dark Ages

It is known that the first coal arrived in Ledbury in March 1798, probably at this wharf, but the Minute Books tell us that it was not until August that Mr. Biddulph was paid "*£272 tor the purchase of his land taken into the Canal, Towing Path, Wharf and Bason at Moat Meadow near Ledbury*". Moat Meadow is on the Ledbury side of the Ross Road and it is likely that this became the main wharf area as shown in maps of the early 19th century.

A wharf cottage stood here on New Street a few yards towards Ledbury on the opposite side of the road to the Biddulph Arms, now the Full Pitcher. In the early 1960's this was still owned by British Railways and Robin Stiles, who purchased the lock cottage at Oxenhall from them, rescued some plans for providing bathroom accommodation for this cottage from a skip. While this building has long gone, the plans give us some idea of the sparse accommodation provided by these old canal cottages.

The pair of cottages which still stand on the South side of the Ross Road may have been part of the wharf there though they are said to date from before the time of the canal.

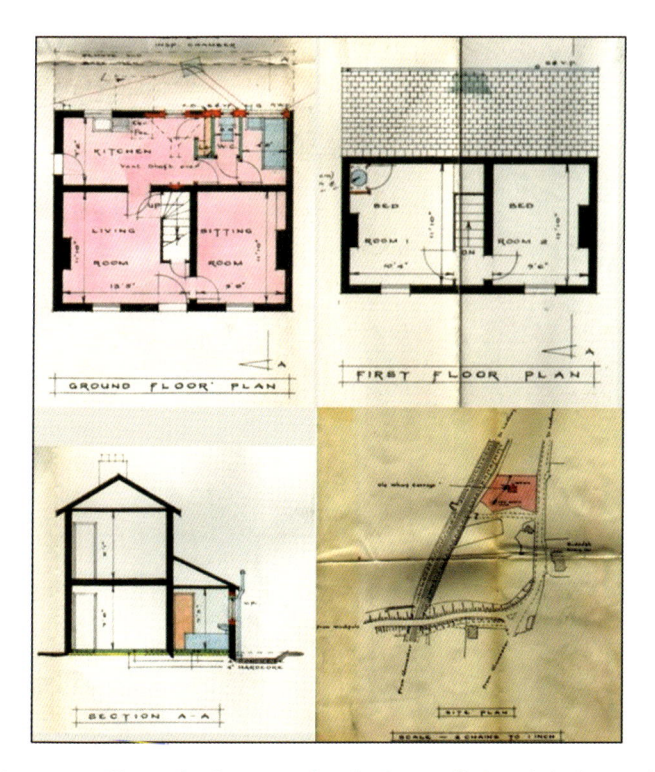

Figure 18: Ledbury Wharf Cottage - Plans for the installation of a bathroom (Robin Stiles)

Dark Ages

Almost all of the 22 locks on the canal completely disappeared, the stone having been incorporated into later buildings and in all probability used by the railway on the Ledbury–Gloucester branch line. The lock at Withington was infilled and probably remains intact in the garden of the lock cottage. There are scant remains at Kymin Lock and some masonry at Over Lock, now buried, but little else. The exception is at Oxenhall where House Lock survived relatively intact, though in a crumbling state. It was listed in 1989, the Official Listing describing it thus:

> *"Lock. c.1795. Designed by Stephen Ballard; engineer, for trustees of the Hereford and Gloucester Canal. Built of limestone ashlar with later brick repairs and stone coping. The gates have decayed. 75 x 8 ft. This is the last surviving lock on the Hereford and Gloucester Canal."*

While the lock cottage is certainly Ballard's work, the lock is not, having been built some nine years before he was born. The gates though, had unquestionably decayed. By 1989 a few fragments were all that remained, enough to make a few "souvenirs" including a small stool which now graces the author's lounge.

Figure 19: The "decayed" gates of House Lock (Mike Potts)

Around 1880 Alfred Watkin's photographed a lock on the canal, which has generally been supposed to be House Lock.

Dark Ages

In recent years, the location of the photograph has been questioned, notably by the late Brian Fox, the Oxenhall restoration Site Leader for many years, who pointed to evidence that the location might be Rudford or Coneybury locks.

Figure 20: Alfred Watkin's photograph, taken about 1880 (Hereford City Library)

The two locks on the River Severn used by boats to reach the Hereford and Gloucester Canal have both survived to the present day. The lock at Maisemore with its lock house was sold by British Waterways in the 1980's to a private owner, but the barge lock and its lock houses at Llanthony was retained, albeit in a steadily deteriorating condition. These are now owned by the Canal Trust.

Figure 21: The narrow Maisemore Lock on the River Severn. This photograph make the lock appear much wider than it actually is, the only narrow lock on the river (Mike Potts)

89

Dark Ages

Other, smaller artefacts lived on, sometimes buried in the accumulated silt or hidden in undergrowth.

The sluice controlling the water from the Canon Frome feeder still exists, and in 2012 with the permission of the landowner, the late Colin Dymott organised an investigation of the feeder itself, assisted by members of the Gloucester Speleological Society. Most of the feeder runs underground through a 4' high tunnel built of local stone, and not brick as was previously thought.

Perhaps even more remarkable is the drainage "plug" at Oxenhall. This has not only survived but was in a state which allowed it to be opened by its leather strap - and were it not for the silted channel below, to fulfil the purpose for which it was designed!

Figure 22: The drainage 'plug' at Oxenhall (Mike Potts)

Where the canal ran along embankments stop gates were fitted to ensure water loss was minimised should a breach occur. These are marked on old Ordnance Survey maps as "Lock" and remarkably one of these survived at least until the mid-1980s. On the Priors Court embankment, near Staplow the unmistakable bulky timbers of a stop gate still in position across the canal, unused for over 100 years, were discovered by members of the Hereford and Gloucester Canal Society – the story of which must shortly be told.

Figure 23: The stop gate on the Priors Court embankment (Mike Potts)

Dark Ages

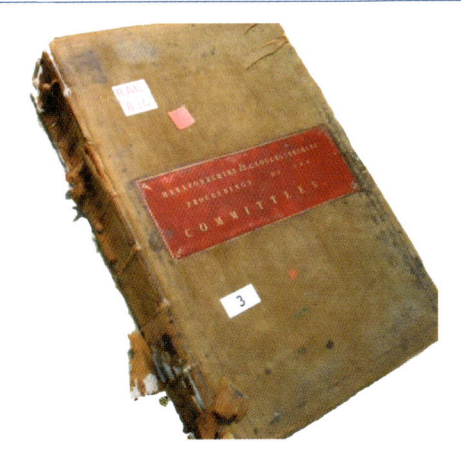

Some documents from the working days of the canal have also been preserved, notably Stephen Ballard's diaries and the Minute Books of the Committee and General Assembly of the Company. Share Registers and other documents and maps are held in the National Archives at Kew and in the Records Offices at Hereford and Gloucester.

Figure 24: One of the Company Minute books in the National Archives (Author)

A number of the original share certificates have also survived, some owned and greatly valued by Trust members. They very occasionally come up for auction.

Figure 25: Share Certificate No. 116 issued to Samuel Carless in 1793 (Nigel Jefferies)

91

A New Beginning

The canal was to sleep for 100 years and it awoke slowly. In 1979 David Bick proposed the restoration of a four-hundred-yard stretch of the canal near Newent Lake and work was actually started, but was soon abandoned on the advice of the Inland Waterways Protection Society.

After a number of letters and articles appeared in local papers a meeting was convened on 13th April 1983 at which the Herefordshire and Gloucestershire Canal Society was inaugurated. The meeting was held at the Red Cross Hall in Hereford, only two hundred yards or so from the site of the terminal Canal Basins. A committee was formed and a number of visits organised to inspect the scant remains of the canal and its associated buildings, the first being to the area around Withington Wharf.

It was agreed that, where possible, cast aluminium plaques should be fixed to some of the important remaining structures, the first being to Widemarsh Bridge in Hereford.

Figure 1: The Mayor of Hereford Cllr. Sim Proctor unveils the plaque on Widemarsh Bridge with Society Chairman Dr. Robin Andrews (kneeling) and David Bick (Mike Potts)

A New Beginning

Figure 2: A poster advertising the inaugural meeting of the Herefordshire and Gloucestershire Canal Society – complete with mis-spelling of Nigel Jefferies name! (Mike Potts)

A New Beginning

Right from the start the Society recognised the need to have good communications with its members, and it soon produced its first newsletter.

HEREFORD AND GLOUCESTER CANAL SOCIETY

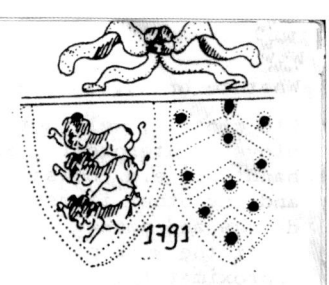

Thankyou for joining the Hereford and Gloucester Canal Society. I hope you will find your membership worthwhile an I look forward to seeing you at the forthcoming events.
We would like to welcome Mr. Robin Andrews as Chairman. Mr. Frank Frecknall is the new Vice Chairman.

MAJOR BARNES ALLOWS CANAL CLEARANCE

Our first canal clearance project is now due to begin on the stretch near Monkhide. Those of you who attended the first canal tour will probably remember the location, with the magnificent Skew Bridge.
The landowner, Major Barnes has kindly agreed to support us in this venture. In fact, Major Barnes has been responsible for gradually clearing the canal by himself for over ten years and was therefore very pleased to hear of the form ation of the Canal Society. He once went as far as getting quote from a contractor's firm for having it dredged. He would like to see the towpath and canal cleared of trees and undergrowth with eventual replanting of trees and wild flow. The north (off) side of the canal will remain untouched. We would like to see this part of the canal returned to an amen ity for both canal enthusiasts and country lovers.
Of course, all we need now are willing helpers! Please read "Working Parties" below:

WORKING PARTIES

The Hereford and Gloucester Canal Society are hoping to hold their first working party on Sunday 3 July at Crews Pit Wharf, nr. Monkhide, on the main Hereford-Worcester road. (A4103)
The work will initially consist of scrub and undergrowth clearance along the towpath side with the aim eventually of more mature trees in the canal bed. All this work will be carried out with the approval and guidance of the landowner.

Figure 3: The first ever newsletter for the Society's members

A New Beginning

There was at this stage no idea of restoring any more than a few short lengths of the canal to show what it might have looked like and if possible, to protect such structures as remained. The first working party descended upon a stretch of the canal adjacent to the main A4103 Hereford to Worcester road at Monkhide, some eight miles by canal from Hereford. This length was owned by Major Robert Barnes, a member of the Society and through his mother, a relation of Stephen Ballard himself.

Figure 4: The first working party at Monkhide in 1983 (Mike Potts)

The stretch included the famous Skew Bridge, possibly the most skewed brick-built bridge built over any canal in Britain. Almost obliterated by ivy and undergrowth, the bridge was exposed, the canal excavated and towpath reinstated. Protection for the bridge was gained by the securing of Grade II listing in January 1986.

The second newsletter, now entitled The Hereford Wharfinger, appeared soon after the work at Monkhide began and included a report on the progress there.

Regular working parties met over the next four years and by 1987 the canal had been cleared from the Hereford to Worcester Road to Skew Bridge. This was only a partial restoration as the full width of the canal was not excavated and the towpath remained considerably higher than the original level, but it demonstrated what could be done.

A New Beginning

Figure 5: The canal at Skew Bridge before restoration began (Mike Potts)

The early working parties were far more informal than they are today. Health and Safety rules were much more relaxed – hard hats were clearly not required and dogs were welcome to lend a hand too.

Figure 6: Early restoration work at Skew Bridge 1983 (Mike Potts)

A New Beginning

Beneath Skew Bridge the towpath had deteriorated considerably and a quantity of hardcore was required to strengthen it. Fortunately, the Society managed to source a free supply which was duly delivered to the site. As it was being broken up fragments of paper were found in it, enough to indicate that the source of the rubble was none other than the demolished Hereford Canal Office which the Society had been unable to save a few months before!

Figure 7: The remains of the canal offices in Hereford, about to form the towpath foundations under Skew Bridge.

By this time enough progress had been made to justify opening the site to the general public and the official opening of this short length of restored canal. The open day was a great success and, much encouraged, the Society began to extend the canal further.

Its achievements and ambitions were recognised by a grant of £2,000 from the Inland Waterways Association.

Figure 8: The presentation of the award from the IWA to the Trust Chairman (left).

A New Beginning

Figure 9: The first Open day of the Canal Society in 1987 (Mike Potts)

Figure 10: Large numbers of people walking the towpath at Monkhide in 1997.
For almost everyone this would have been their first visit to the canal (Gordon Lothian)

There was, at this stage, no public admission that the Society harboured any aspirations to restore the whole canal to full navigation, though some of its members were privately beginning to develop such a vision and the Society's Committee began to debate whether a change of policy should be made.

A New Beginning

This was at least partly at the suggestion of both the Hereford and Worcester and the Gloucestershire County Councils. David Bick, a member of the Committee sought advice from Charles Hadfield, one of the country's leading authorities on canals, a co-founder of the Inland Waterways Association and vice-president of three canal restoration societies. Hadfield's advice was unequivocal and not encouraging.

In a letter to Bick dated January 12th 1988 Hadfield lists a whole host of reasons why restoration of the Hereford and Gloucester was a completely ridiculous idea. He listed issues of huge cost, both of restoration and maintenance, the time it would take and the fact that so little of the original canal remained. What about landowners, water supply and access from the Severn now that Maisemore lock had been sold?

And who would want to cruise it anyway, well away from the main cruising areas and a dead end?

He concludes his advice to David Bick thus:

These are a few of the obvious objections. All round the country lie the wrecks of good intentions – The Thames & Severn, the Portsmouth and Arundel, the Wey and Arun, the Grantham (in spite of being a BWB canal) etc. etc. They finish up as a hobby of a few dozen enthusiasts who potter about in wellies in a lock here and there, and pretend to themselves that they are doing good, when all they are doing – to be blunt – is to inflate their egos.

"My suggestion is that you have nothing to do with it. Resign from the Society, and form an amenity group to work with the local authorities on (a) preserving important structures as they are; (b) putting up informative historical notices; (c) issuing a trail guide for school and tourist use and a series of trail walks led by experts; and so on. In other words, keep the memory of the canal alive but do no restoration. The Americans are very good at this ..."

Charles Hadfield in a letter to David Bick January 12th 1988

Since these words were written the few dozen enthusiasts in their wellies has grown to many hundreds, raising and spending many millions of pounds and making great strides in restoring many derelict waterways. Hadfield would have been delighted, but at the time, he undoubtedly raised some very important issues, which might well have convinced the Society that full restoration was, indeed, out of the question.

But for the second time in the canal's history, optimism triumphed over pragmatism and privately, at least, the Society began to change its aims. Although David Bick shared Hadfield's view that full restoration was impossible, he remained a member of the Society and Trust to the end of his life.

By 1990 the Society was openly speaking of full restoration and attended the Inland Waterways Festival at Gloucester with a large stand and display which won many new members to the Society, including the present author.

The canal was forced further into public notice in the following year when proposals were published for a Hereford bypass to be built on the eastern side of the city. This would have cut through the Lugg Meadows, the largest and most important Lammas Meadows in England and a Site of Special Scientific Interest. For the Canal Society, more to the point, it would run across the line of the canal preventing it from ever reaching Hereford. To oppose construction of the bypass without provision for the canal was valid only if full restoration between Hereford and Gloucester was a realistic possibility.

The original proposals had rejected a canal crossing on the basis of cost. At the Public Enquiry the Society's Chairman, a civil engineer by profession, argued that the Department of Transport's costs for a navigable culvert were double what they should have been and that a number of other false assumptions had been made. After an adjournment the Inspector recommended that provision for the canal should be made, a decision accepted by the Department of Transport.

Over 30 years later Hereford is still waiting for its bypass, but the argument had been won and an important stake had been driven into the ground. Of almost equal importance, the cat was now completely out of the bag. The Society intended to restore the entire canal to full navigation.

In the same year, 1991, Robin Stiles, the owner of House Lock at Oxenhall near Newent allowed members of the Society to begin clearance of the lock site. This was important, as hitherto all restoration work had been carried out in Herefordshire and the Committee was concerned to have a restoration site in both counties.

While House Lock was the only one on the canal where there was anything much to see, it was in a very sorry state indeed. Much of the stonework had crumbled away and there was a prolific growth of trees rising from the base of the chamber. It was a sad and daunting prospect.

A New Beginning

Figure 11: House Lock, Oxenhall almost hidden under years of vegetation growth (Mike Potts)

The following year the Society took an important step forward when it became registered as a Charitable Trust, now with the clearly stated aim of restoring the canal from its junction with the River Severn at Over to the centre of the City of Hereford.

Work in earnest was about to begin.

The Herefordshire and Gloucestershire Canal Trust

While the transition from Society to Charitable Trust in 1992 made little outward appearance it gave significant advantages, opening up new ways of securing grant aid for restoration and equipment and putting things on a more secure legal footing. The establishment of Herefordshire and Gloucestershire Canal (Sales), a not-for-profit Trading Company associated with the Trust also opened up new possibilities.

It was essential in these early days to develop the identity and ethos of the Trust, building on what had already been established by the Canal Society. The original Company seal made an ideal logo, reproduced in black on yellow. Trust members working on display stands at external events became easily recognisable by their yellow and black sweatshirts. A large yellow flag bearing the Company seal flew over their stand at outdoor events.

With a steadily growing sense of self-confidence, it was essential to reinforce the professionalism of the Trust. There was a determination that, whatever the Trust attempted to do, it must do it well. This extended far beyond work on the canal itself – it was to apply across the board, from rigorous financial management, high quality publicity material and excellence in the Trust's quarterly magazine, The Wharfinger.

Figure 1: The flag and official logo (Janet Moult)

Health and Safety was established as being of paramount importance, not only for restoration work but covering all the activities of the Trust and the Trading Company. Comprehensive policies and protocols were developed, regularly reviewed and followed as a matter of course.

The threats to the canal experienced in Herefordshire indicated that the first priority for the Trust must be to convince the Local Authorities of the need to

The Herefordshire and Gloucestershire Canal Trust

protect the line of the canal from any developments which could compromise restoration, however far in the future that might be. Local government is subject to reorganisation from time to time and it was vital to ensure that the protection afforded to the canal corridor was carried through from one body to its successor. The short-lived county of Hereford and Worcester was abolished in 1998 and Herefordshire re-established as a unitary authority. The campaigning carried out by the Society to protect the canal under Hereford and Worcester had to be reiterated for the new authority, with the resulting following robust planning policy:

> *RST 9 Herefordshire and Gloucestershire Canal*
>
> *The historic route of the Herefordshire and Gloucestershire Canal together with its associated infrastructure, buildings, towpath and features will be safeguarded. Where the original alignment cannot be re-established, a corridor allowing for deviations is safeguarded. New developments within the safeguarded corridor, or on adjacent sites, will be required to incorporate land for the Canal restoration. Development not connected with the Canal that would prevent or prejudice the restoration of a continuous route will not be permitted.*
>
> *Herefordshire Council: Herefordshire Unitary Development Plan March 2007*

Most of the canal in Gloucestershire lies within the Forest of Dean District Council and this also adopted a policy protecting the canal, supported by the following narrative:

> *Considerable effort has already resulted in the restoration of several sections of the canal and it is important that the ultimate reinstatement is not compromised by development. The Plan will therefore safeguard the historic line of the Canal where it is not already obstructed by permanent structures. Where so obstructed, the Council will safeguard any agreed diversion routes. The Plan will therefore safeguard the route of the canal and shall seek to ensure its restoration as part of any adjacent development.*
>
> *The Forest of Dean District Local Plan Review, 2005*

Subsequent revisions to planning policies have maintained or strengthened these safeguards. While striving to secure the protection of the canal it was easy to see property development as the enemy and planning objections where restoration was threatened, an automatic response. However, it soon became apparent that working with developers rather than against them was a much more effective way forward.

The Herefordshire and Gloucestershire Canal Trust

In particular, agreements under Section 106 of the Town and Country Planning Act (1990) by which developments could be permitted subject to making the associated canal land available or even providing the funding for restoration along it, were found to be invaluable. Over only the first few years of the Trust's existence a number of spectacularly successful agreements were reached securing millions of pounds worth of investment in the canal.

But undoubtedly the greatest difficulty facing the new Trust in restoring the entire canal was that it owned none of it. Following the closure of the canal in 1881 the Proprietors attempted to get what they could for the parts of the canal line not used by the railway. In some cases, they could scarcely give it away, but retrieving it from the present owners was never going to be easy. However, it was important that there was visible progress towards eventual restoration and therefore, like other similar projects elsewhere, this would have to take the form of the restoration of short lengths of canal, the property of sympathetic land-owners, as opportunities arose.

Volunteer teams were set up at each site as it became available. A designated Site Leader managed the work programme within an agreed budget. While often the Site Leader and some of the volunteers were initially associated with an existing site, in each case a new site brought new volunteers, usually local people attracted by the challenge of worthwhile voluntary work and the opportunity to join a team of like-minded people. Rapidly the teams developed their own identity and, with training always being provided, their own skills.

The Trust also recognised from the start that simply restoring the canal was not enough to secure its future. It had to be able to generate sufficient income to support the on-going maintenance costs of operating the canal. Sustainability, both financial and ecological, became a key element in the Trust's thinking and working, constantly exploring ways in which income could be maximised, expenditure minimised and a positive approach to environmental issues adopted.

Experience of other waterways, including those owned by British Waterways (now the Canal and River Trust) was that income from the paying users of the canal, principally boating licenses, mooring fees, and rental from canal-based businesses would never be adequate. Most people visiting canals do so on foot and therefore more imaginative ways have to be found to generate sufficient revenue. Over time this meant that the Trust had to spend some of its hard-won resources on securing income for the future rather than on restoring the canal itself. These were investments that simply had to be made to ensure a long-term future for the canal.

The Herefordshire and Gloucestershire Canal Trust

Consideration of the wider economic aspects was also important. The benefits of a fully restored canal to the local community through which it passes are many and varied, but the impact on the local economy is a vital factor in securing support from the local authorities, grant awarding bodies, potential sponsors and the public. British Waterways carried out a study of the canal in 1995 using comparative data from similar operational waterways and estimated an additional local spend resulting from the canal of £6 million per year.

A further study in 2009 updated this figure to £20 million, the increase relating to both inflation and the increased tourism engagement with canals and added an estimate of extra jobs created at some 500 full time equivalents. It is anticipated that the continued growth of the Trust's ambitions, looking at the broader corridor of the canal rather than just the canal itself, will see an increase in these estimates. Early evidence from numerous sources indicates that during the Covid-19 pandemic the public's use and appreciation of green spaces such as woodland, parks and waterways increased markedly and it is thought that much of this effect may be sustained long after the pandemic has passed.

Other key principles and activities were carried forward from the Canal Society including raising awareness and public support. The membership of the Trust had to be built up and maintained, for this is a measure of public support for the restoration, a key determinant in the eyes of funding bodies. In those early days the very existence of the old canal was still unknown to a great many people, even to those living close to its original line.

A Trading Company was established which took stands at all major waterway and many local events and continues to have a busy programme during the summer months – sometimes having to split its resources over more than one event on the same day.

Figure 2: The Trust stand at a national event in 2010 (Janet Moult)

Figure 3: The Trust's Winter Fayre at Newent Memorial Hall 2022 (Author)

A programme of monthly Social Evenings, generally with an invited speaker, was soon established and has been well supported ever since. Trust members gave talks to groups both in the two counties and further afield and still do so, though now the interest is more in progress towards restoration than discovering the canal itself. Tours of the canal were arranged from time-to-time visiting restoration sites and other points of interest.

From the earliest days of the Canal Society, it's quarterly magazine for members, beginning as a simple newsletter in 1983, has been an important way to promote the canal, publicise events and keep members informed of new developments. The name The Wharfinger had been used from the second edition onwards, but it was not until Edition 115, in Spring 2013, that the words "Rebuilding 34 miles of canal between Gloucester and Hereford" appeared on the front cover, leaving the reader in no doubt of the objectives of the Trust. The Wharfinger is now widely regarded as one of the best journals produced by any canal trust or society.

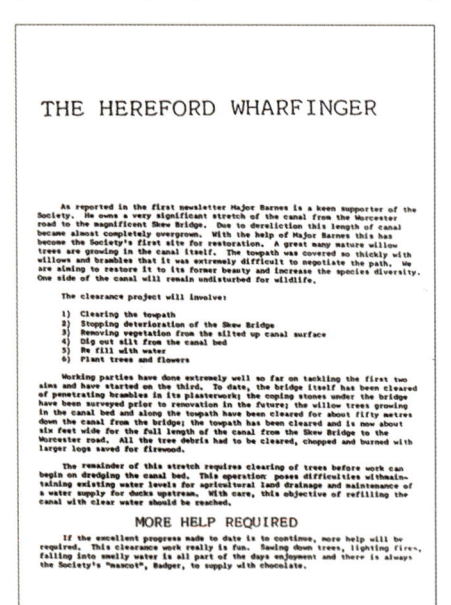

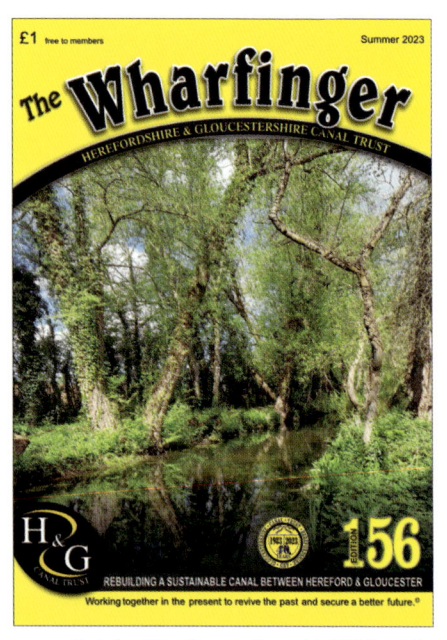

Figure 4: The second edition of the newsletter, now called the Wharfinger, alongside Edition 156 published in Summer 2023

The Trust also accepted from an early stage that it could not restore 34 miles of canal on its own. This would have to be done in close partnership with other bodies and organisations which shared the vision of the restored canal. In particular, working with local authorities and with developers would prove essential. It looked for, and found, support from the Inland Waterways Association (IWA) and the Waterway Recovery Group (WRG) the huge contribution of which will be told in following pages.

An essential partnership in all canal restorations is with the Environment Agency (EA). Water supply for any canal is essential, and this is a significant issue for a canal with many locks as all boat movements result in the removal to the lower level of a lock full of water – close to 200 tons in the case of the Hereford & Gloucester Canal's locks. An independent study on water supply and management for the Canal was commissioned jointly by the Trust and the EA and carried out by Birmingham University's School of Civil Engineering between 1996 and 2001, drawing on data from British Waterways, the EA and other sources, as well as considerations of the rivers, catchment areas and countryside through which the Canal will pass. This concluded that the foreseeable demands of the fully restored Canal would be met adequately from a combination of some historic sources, specific identified new sources and water conservation measures including back pumping. These conclusions now form the basis of the Trust's overall plan for water for the restored canal.

As the Trust matured these basic principles were developed and enhanced. Lessons would be learnt, sometimes painfully, but the foundations have proved to be sound.

In recent years a Canal Festival at Over basin has been held, when the basin has been thronged with people enjoying the waterside and a whole range of activities including cruises on Mister Maysey, the Trust's trip boat, a procession of the Trust's heritage boats, a horse-drawn boat, classic cars and the handiwork of the members of the Gloucester and District Model Boat Club. There were craft and produce stalls, great food and beer, cider and perry.

Figure 5: 'Alder' leads a procession of boats at the 2012 Over Canal Festival with Timothy West and Prunella Scales, strong supporters of the Trust, on the bow deck (Ted Beagles)

The Herefordshire and Gloucestershire Canal Trust

HEREFORDSHIRE & GLOUCESTERSHIRE CANAL TRUST — 30p

Working *together* in the present, to revive the past, and secure a better future.

CANAL WALK NO. 3
DYMOCK

This walk starts at Dymock, Gloucestershire, which is about four miles north of Newent, on the B4215. Grid ref: 701312

Parking: There is a lay-by opposite the Beauchamp Arms in Dymock, but it can only accommodate three cars. Additional parking is to the north of the village, beside the old road to Maypole Farm, opposite the close named The Crypt.
Distance: 5 miles
Time: 1½ hours (approx.)

Figure 6: Dymock Walk leaflet

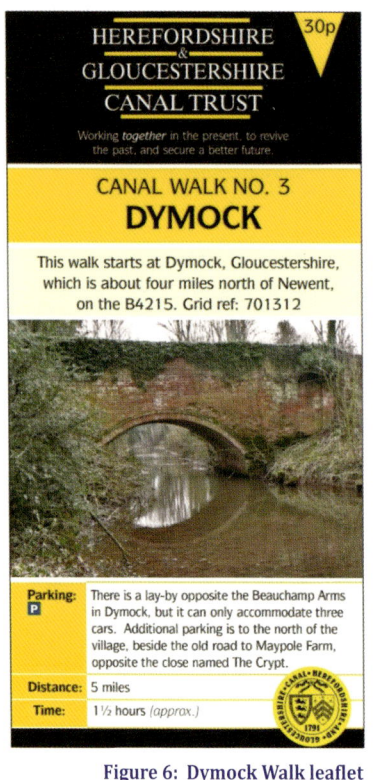

It is not intended that such gatherings will be limited to Over in the future. As restoration of the canal progresses gatherings with held at new sites with fresh opportunities for people to enjoy themselves on or by the water.

Although almost the whole of the canal lies in private land and many parts of it are not easily accessible, the Trust has produced a series of attractive leaflets describing mostly circular walks along footpaths and such lengths of the towpath where this is possible.

Each leaflet describes the route of the walk and the places of interest along the canal. Eight leaflets are now available covering areas around Staplow, Withington, Dymock, Llanthony Lock, Oxenhall, Over, Ashperton and Ledbury. Since almost the whole of the canal line passes through attractive countryside, these walk leaflets have proved very popular. There are well researched and provide an interesting background to the walk itself.

In June 2022 the Herefordshire Walking Festival included a 7½ walk, much of it along the canal towpath at Yarkhill and Monkhide, including a stop by the canal for a picnic lunch. This walk included stretches of the towpath where the landowner gave permission for the towpath to be used for this occasion which are not normally open to the public.

In 2015 the Trust launched its 225 Anniversary Campaign, both celebrating the 225th anniversary of the formation of the original canal company and looking forward to the future. A major theme of the campaign was reinforcing the need to acquire the land that had been sold or given away when the canal closed. A major launch event was held at Eastnor Castle, built with stone carried along the canal in 1810 and now the home of James Hervey-Bathurst, a Trust Vice-President. Guests at this private event included Dame Janet Trotter, the Lord Lieutenant of Gloucestershire and Christopher James DL representing the Countess of Darnley, Lord Lieutenant of Herefordshire.

The Herefordshire and Gloucestershire Canal Trust

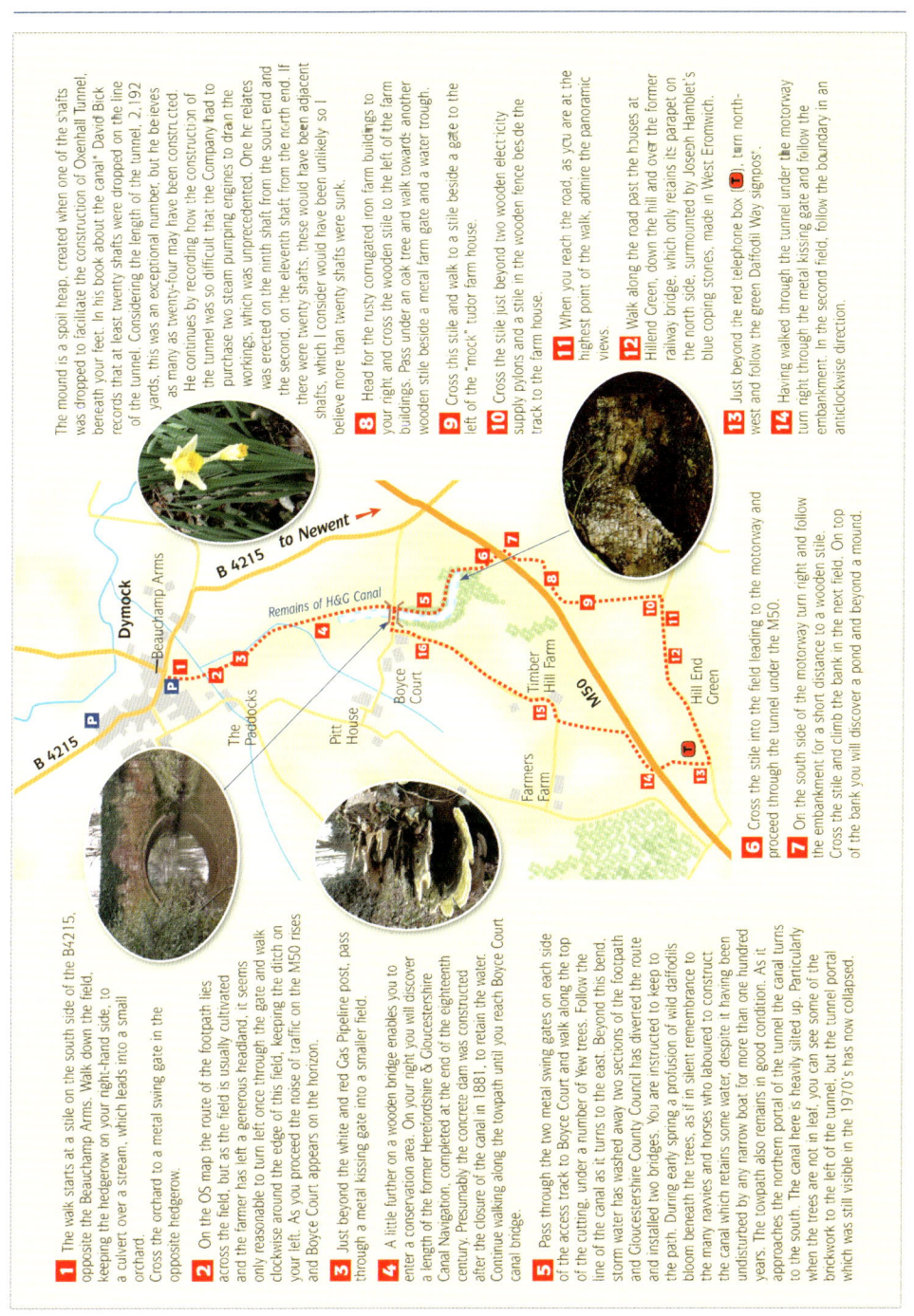

1 The walk starts at a stile on the south side of the B4215, opposite the Beauchamp Arms. Walk down the field, keeping the hedgerow on your right-hand side, to a culvert over a stream, which leads into a small orchard.
Cross the orchard to a metal swing gate in the opposite hedgerow.

2 On the OS map the route of the footpath lies across the field, but as the field is usually cultivated and the farmer has left a generous headland, it seems only reasonable to turn left once through the gate and walk clockwise around the edge of this field, keeping the ditch on your left. As you proceed the noise of traffic on the M50 rises and Boyce Court appears on the horizon.

3 Just beyond the white and red Gas Pipeline post, pass through a metal kissing gate into a smaller field.

4 A little further on a wooden bridge enables you to enter a conservation area. On your right you will discover a length of the former Herefordshire & Gloucestershire Canal Navigation, completed at the end of the eighteenth century. Presumably the concrete dam was constructed after the closure of the canal in 1881, to retain the water.
Continue walking along the towpath until you reach Boyce Court canal bridge.

5 Pass through the two metal swing gates on each side of the access track to Boyce Court and walk along the top of the cutting, under a number of Yew trees. Follow the line of the canal as it turns to the east. Beyond this bend, storm water has washed away two sections of the footpath and Gloucestershire County Council has diverted the route and installed two bridges. You are instructed to keep to the path. During early spring a profusion of wild daffodils bloom beneath the trees, as if in silent remembrance to the many navvies and horses who laboured to construct the canal which retains some water, despite it having been undisturbed by any narrow boat for more than one hundred years. The towpath also remains in good condition. As it approaches the northern portal of the tunnel the canal turns to the south. The canal here is heavily silted up. Particularly when the trees are not in leaf, you can see some of the brickwork to the left of the tunnel, but the tunnel portal which was still visible in the 1970's has now collapsed.

The mound is a spoil heap, created when one of the shafts was dropped to facilitate the construction of Oxenhall Tunnel, beneath your feet. In his book about the canal" David Bick records that at least twenty shafts were dropped on the line of the tunnel. Considering the length of the tunnel, 2,192 yards, this was an exceptional number, but he believes as many as twenty-four may have been constructed.
He continues by recording how the construction of the tunnel was so difficult that the Company had to purchase two steam pumping engines to drain the workings, which was unprecedented. One he relates was erected on the ninth shaft from the south end and the second, on the eleventh shaft from the north end. If there were twenty shafts, these would have been adjacent shafts, which I consider would have been unlikely so I believe more than twenty shafts were sunk.

6 Cross the stile into the field leading to the motorway and proceed through the tunnel under the M50.

7 On the south side of the motorway turn right and follow the embankment for a short distance to a wooden stile. Cross the stile and climb the bank in the next field. On top of the bank you will discover a pond and beyond a mound.

8 Head for the rusty corrugated iron farm buildings to your right and cross the wooden stile to the left of the farm buildings. Pass under an oak tree and walk towards another wooden stile beside a metal farm gate and a water trough.

9 Cross this stile and walk to a stile beside a gate to the left of the "mock" tudor farm house.

10 Cross the stile just beyond two wooden electricity supply pylons and a stile in the wooden fence beside the track to the farm house.

11 When you reach the road, as you are at the highest point of the walk, admire the panoramic views.

12 Walk along the road past the houses at Hillend Green, down the hill and over the former railway bridge, which only retains its parapet on the north side, surmounted by Joseph Hamblet's blue coping stones, made in West Bromwich.

13 Just beyond the red telephone box (B), turn north-west and follow the green Daffodil Way signposts.

14 Having walked through the tunnel under the motorway turn right through the metal kissing gate and follow the embankment. In the second field, follow the boundary in an anticlockwise direction.

Figure 7: Inside of the Dymock Walk leaflet

The Herefordshire and Gloucestershire Canal Trust

Speakers included Richard Parry, Chief Executive of the Canal and River Trust. A Land Fund was established to attract donations from as many sources as possible including individual benefactors, corporate sponsors, statutory funders, grant-making trusts and gifts from the wider community.

Also in 2015, observant readers of Edition 124 of The Wharfinger would have noticed that a new logo appeared, not on the cover, but on one of the inside pages. This was to replace the original, rather complicated logo based on the Company Seal. The new logo was of a much simpler, more eye-catching, design featuring a remarkable approximation to the line of the canal, wending its way between the two Cities.

Figure 8: The New Logo

On April 6th 2016 the Trust received the news that it had been awarded the Queen's Award for Voluntary Service. It was hard to keep this a secret until June 2nd, the late Queen's birthday when the news embargo was lifted. One of the main demonstrations of the achievements of the Trust's volunteers had been shown to the Deputy Lieutenants of both counties on a visit to Over Basin, rebuilt almost entirely by volunteers at a cost of £65,000 instead of the £750,000 quoted by contractors.

Figure 9: Janet Moult - Chairman, receives the award on behalf of the Trust from Air Vice Marshal Mike Smart DL (Photo Glow)

On July 13th the award was presented to the Trust at Over Basin by Dame Janet Trotter, Lord Lieutenant of Gloucestershire. Air Vice Marshal Mike Smart

The Herefordshire and Gloucestershire Canal Trust

DL, represented the Countess of Darnley, Lord Lieutenant of Herefordshire. Before the presentation the representatives of HM The Queen enjoyed a trip along the canal aboard Alder.

Part of the award's citation read:

> *"The Herefordshire and Gloucestershire Canal Trust is an exceptionally well organised and managed group of dedicated volunteers which has been working ever since 1992 to restore this 34-mile Canal which joins Hereford with the navigable River Severn at Gloucester. The Trust and its remarkable volunteers in both counties are achieving substantial benefits for local communities. This is a vibrant and thriving example of the power of volunteering. we have no hesitation in recommending it for a Queen's Award for Voluntary Service."*

By 2018 most of the members of the Trust's Board of Trustees had served continuously for many years – in several cases, decades. Some had reluctantly resigned through ill health or personal reasons and others did not seek re-election. Over the following two years new members were elected to the Board but the departure of those who had given so much of their time and energy and had accumulated vast amounts of local knowledge, created a great vacuum. However, the Board now had a new and wide range of professional experience and expertise and was able to begin to look at things in new ways.

While ever-mindful of the need for sustainability to be a vital strand of its restoration strategy, reflecting the focus of the Anniversary Campaign efforts were concentrated on the acquisition of land wherever this was possible and on the opening of new lengths of canal.

The arrival of the Covid-19 pandemic early in 2020 resulted in a near total shut down of the Trust's public and collaborative activities. But there was still much which could be done by volunteers at home - design work, writing letters, making grant applications and dealing with the matters of corporate governance which are necessary for the proper running of a charitable trust. Committees continued to meet, but online rather than in person.

This was a frustrating time for those with work to do outdoors who were prevented from working with others by the Covid lock-down regulations and working alone by the Trust's Health and Safety rules. It was not until the Spring of 2021 that anything like the Trust's normal activities were able to restart, and it did so with renewed vigour.

Restoration in Herefordshire

Returning to our story of the Canal itself, following the formation of the Trust, work on the canal at Monkhide continued apace and in 1992 another open event was held – this time an Open Weekend, drawing large numbers of people with a variety of attractions alongside the canal. Trip boats, including one of the very first fibre-glass cruisers ever to use this canal, gave the public a taste of being afloat on their own local waterway.

Figure 1: The busy open day at Monkhide in 1992 (Mike Potts)

The late Sir John Knill, one of the last regular commercial carriers on British canals, had given the Trust Mallard, a wood and fibreglass work boat which had been refurbished and provided with an outboard motor. Major Barnes' own trip boat Brindley was also in service, these boats mingling with canoes, a coracle and a steam launch.

A brass band, Morris dancers, demonstrations of country crafts, plenty of food and displays promoting the restoration of the canal kept visitors busy for the whole weekend. For many of the visitors this was the first inkling that there had ever been a canal in Herefordshire.

Restoration in Herefordshire

Figure 2: The Trust's Trip Boat 'Mallard' in the glorious sunshine of the 1992 Open Weekend (Mike Potts)

Figure 3: Sir Ivor, one of the first glass-fibre cruisers ever to use the Hereford and Gloucester Canal serves as a trip boat at the Open Weekend in 1992 (Mike Potts)

Despite the publicity the canal was now receiving and the Inspector's decision in the bypass enquiry, when the Hereford and Worcester County Council carried out their Roman Road improvements in 1995 they planned to culvert the canal beneath the road once again threatening to prevent the canal ever reaching the centre of Hereford, though tantalisingly within arm's reach. The

Restoration in Herefordshire

Trust successfully challenged this decision and the County Council funded the £100,000 navigable culvert to allow boats to reach Hereford at some point in the future. The concrete culvert has little of the charm of Ballard's old canal bridge, but was designed for a stonework facing to be added in the future.

More importantly, another vital battle had been won.

Figure 4: Stephen Ballard's Roman Road Bridge and it's concrete replacement (Mike Potts and Cliff Penny)

Another Open Weekend was held in 1995 and once again this was a great success with many visitors, both local and from further afield. To celebrate the opening of a further length of the canal Major Barnes had his narrow boat Maria Ballard, named after Stephen Ballard's wife, transported from its home mooring at Worcester and for the first time cruised Ballard's canal. There was a display of vintage cars and other attractions and the Society's Trading Company had displays about the canal and sold various items in order to raise money towards further restoration.

Figure 5: Vintage cars at the Monkhide Open Day 1995 (Mike Potts)

Restoration in Herefordshire

Figure 6: The narrow boat 'Maria Ballard' leads a procession of boats along the newly restored length of canal at the Monkhide Canal Open Weekend 1995 (Mike Potts)

While restoration at Monkhide had been carried out in association with the landowner there was no legal agreement between the two parties, and in particular, any arrangement by which the public could be guaranteed unrestricted access to the restored canal.

A similar situation existed in Gloucestershire on the lengths approaching Oxenhall Tunnel. As the restoration had been carried out mainly by volunteers and funded by public donations, this was a situation unacceptable to the Trust. It directly led to the adoption of a fundamental principle that it would only allow restoration work to commence on sites that it owned, or were the subject of a legal agreement which guaranteed access for restoration and, when complete, for maintenance and enjoyment by the general public.

In consequence, although major preliminary restoration works were completed on these sites there has not been any further restoration or significant maintenance undertaken by the Trust at any site which the Trust does not own or where appropriate legal agreements are not in place. There has not been an open day at Monkhide since 1995.

Restoration in Herefordshire

Figure 7: Stephen Ballard's magnificent Skew Bridge at Monkhide in 2002

Figure 8: Middlecourt Bridge on the partly restored Monkhide section of the canal (Author)

In November 1994 a legal agreement was reached between the Trust and the owner of Whitwick Manor in relation to a stretch of canal at Yarkhill some 1000 yards long on the northern side of the A4103. This led to, but did not include, the site of Barrs Lock, the first of the three locks which lowered the canal towards Hereford.

Restoration in Herefordshire

A major clearance of the site began immediately and excavation of the canal and grading of the towpath was carried out in the autumn by a major work camp. Though plagued by extremely wet weather, great progress was made and after further work the following year the canal filled with water from natural drainage of adjoining streams. Although not part of the site, with the neighbour's agreement, a trial excavation was carried out to determine the exact position of the lock. Nothing was found – either the excavation was not deep enough, in the wrong place, or no stone or brickwork remained.

This length of the canal includes no bridges or other structures requiring restoration, but the canal bed and banks had been badly damaged by the growth of large trees which had to be removed. Consequently, while the stretch held water well in winter, in summer, with evaporation and little feed from land drainage it could dry up completely.

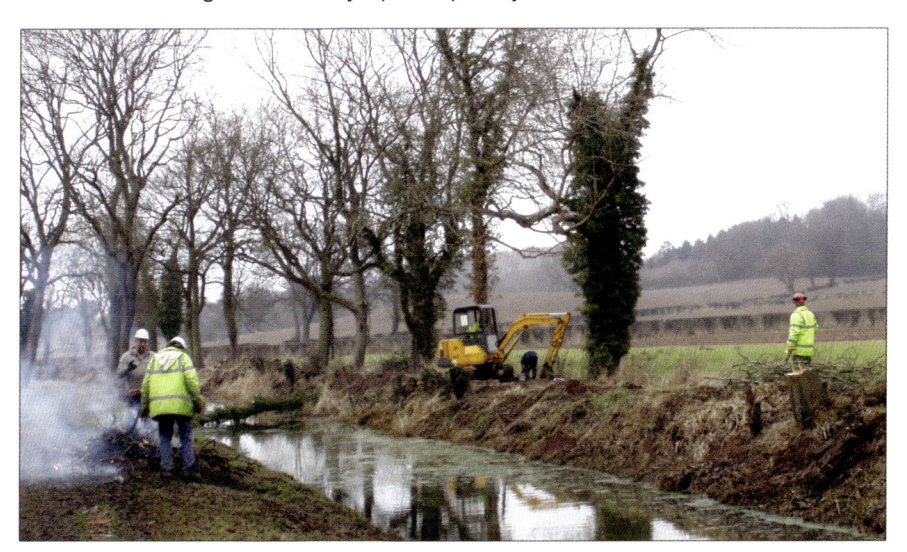

Figure 9: Tree and stump clearance being carried out at Yarkhill (Chris High)

In 2005 a new restoration team was formed with some help from the Waterway Recovery Group, and has done much to bring the site up to a high standard. A great number of tree stumps have been removed and considerable work still needs to be done to restore the original profile. Some leaks have been sealed including the excavation of the canal bed at the Barrs Lock end to repair a hole in the culvert that passes under the canal but more work is necessary to make it watertight. This is a difficult and time-consuming task.

Encouraged by the Site Leader, the towpath, despite the remote location, is now used and much appreciated by local people.

Figure 10: The canal at Yarkhill in 2008 (Chris High)

Informal Open Days have been held when large numbers of people walked the towpath, but the remote location, the want of a slipway and lack of water during the summer makes it impractical to hold major public events here.

In 2008 a replica of milestone 27, carved by Trust volunteers, was erected by the canal, the first of the new set of milestones which will be required to replace all those which have been lost.

Figure 11: Replica Milestone 27 (Author)

With the permission of the owner, further excavation work has also been carried out, at the site of Barrs Lock on a slightly different alignment, this time with considerable success. While little evidence of the stone or brickwork of the lock walls has been found, masonry at the bottom of the lock has been discovered and brickwork forming the bottom offside corner and lock invert uncovered.

Restoration in Herefordshire

Figure 12: Excavation of Barrs Lock revealing some of the remaining masonry and brickwork
(Chris High)

In 2012 agreement was reached with the owner of the land between Barrs Lock and Kymin to restore 1,000 yards of canal. This is adjacent to the Yarkhill stretch already under restoration and has the advantage of road access at The Kymin. Being a heavily wooded stretch, the restoration is designed to retain as many trees as possible, such that from the surrounding countryside the landscape will appear little changed. Work began in November with the Waterway Recovery Group National Reunion Weekend when over 100 "WRGies" descended on the site and begun to clear the line to be restored. About 800 yards were cleared, the remaining 200 being dealt with in two weekends by Trust volunteers early in 2013.

Although much scrub and some trees had to be removed, over 150 new trees have been planted as part of the restoration. During the summer of the same year final site clearance was undertaken, tree stumps removed and a drainage channel dug to drain water away from the canal itself to allow the excavation work to be carried out the following year.

Although much dryer than the previous year, two dumpers and an excavator got stuck in the mud. By the autumn, 650 yards of canal and towpath were completed. Four land drains run into the canal which will not only help to drain the surrounding area but will keep the new stretch of canal topped up with water.

Restoration in Herefordshire

Figure 13: The new length of the canal at Kymin in 2015 (Wilf Jones)

The Kymin East section of the canal is one of the 'lower profile' sites currently being worked on as it is only easily accessed from one of Herefordshire's typical country lanes, apparently miles from anywhere.

The canal passes through a very wooded area with many well-established trees, as many as possible of which were left untouched by the restoration work. The wet surroundings encourage very active growth of vegetation and hence much of the work at the site is keeping this in check and dealing with trees uprooted by recent major storms in the area.

In 2020 a limited amount of work was carried on the stretch of canal immediately north of the A4103, Hereford-Worcester trunk road. This is continuous with, but not part of, the Yarkhill section. A number of trees which had fallen across the canal were successfully removed, together with general scrub overgrowth.

Figure 14: Walkers enjoy the Kymin stretch of the towpath on a Canal Walk day in June 2020 (Ralph Barber)

Restoration in Herefordshire

On the strength of the quality of this work the landowner allowed work to be carried out on the section of the canal at Monkhide that had been restored 30 years ago and the site of the Open Weekends in 1992 and 1995, but had lain largely untouched since.

The total length of the canal between Kymin and Monkhide is about two miles. For this to become a fully navigable section Barr's Lock will have to be rebuilt and a new bridge constructed to carry the main Hereford-Worcester road over the canal. While the lock can be rebuilt using volunteers at a fraction of the cost of involving contractors, the road crossing will inevitably involve the highway authority and a very good case will have to be established before this work would be approved, but the engineering requirements present no great challenges.

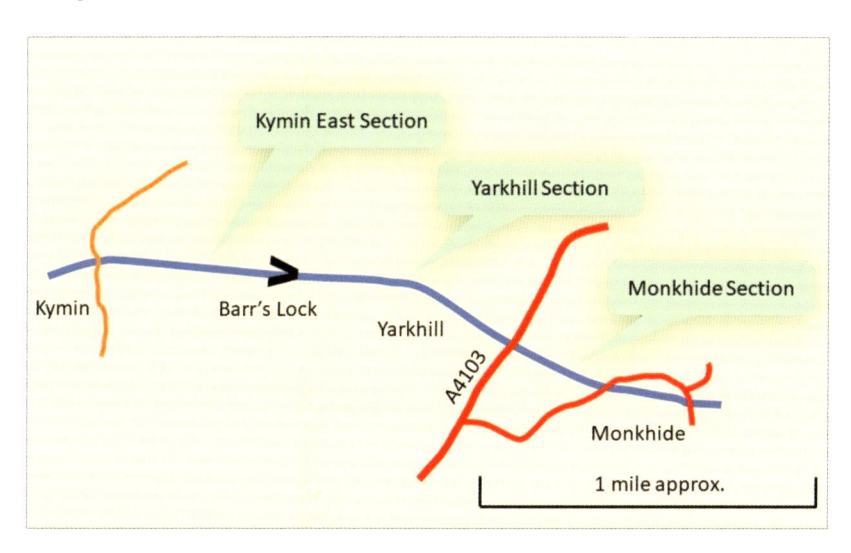

Figure 15: The three restoration sites between Kymin and Monkhide

Some five miles towards Hereford, on the outskirts of the City itself, another length of canal had become available for restoration in 2002 following the acquisition by the Herefordshire Council of a considerable area of land adjoining Aylestone Hill for development into a public park. The line of the canal ran along the northern edge of the site. One of the first tasks was to build a compound to securely house the paraphernalia required to carry out work on the site. This was done in association with the Waterway Recovery Group in the most appalling, freezing cold wind. Such is the devotion of the restorers of canals! Work on scrub clearance and tree felling followed in preparation for the excavation of a quarter of a mile of canal.

Restoration in Herefordshire

Figure 16: Brian Moult, Chair of the Trading Company, scrub-bashing at Aylestone Park. Sadly, Brian died the following morning. (Keith Kitson)

The canal itself had not been infilled but had accumulated a large quantity of silt almost to the level of the surrounding ground. There had been factories bordering the canal, including a tile works and many years ago it had been the custom to dispose of unwanted paints and other materials into the canal. After the author had given a talk about the canal in Hereford and spoken of this, an elderly gentleman introduced himself and, much embarrassed, confessed that, as a boy of about 15, this had been his job at the end of his working day!

Preliminary tests had shown the silt to be uncontaminated and a Waterway Recovery Group work-camp was planned for Easter 2004. However, further tests carried out shortly before the camp indicated significant levels of contamination by heavy metals. The camp was cancelled and the Trust Council faced the challenge of how to excavate and dispose of many tons of contaminated silt.

The transportation and disposal of this material is extremely expensive – far beyond the budget of the Trust at the time. The solution was found within the park itself, where a number of roadways and parking areas were to be constructed. In 2007 Celtic Technologies excavated 1,800 cubic metres of silt from the canal which was processed on site to create a solid, inert compound from which the contaminants cannot leach and this formed the foundations of these hard areas.

Restoration in Herefordshire

Figure 17: The removal of contaminated silt from the canal in 2007

Once the silt had been removed a partial restoration of the canal could be undertaken.

Figure 18: The partly restored canal in Aylestone Park (Author)

In May 2011 the first Boat Gathering was held following the completion of a slipway. This was one of the landmark events in the history of the canal's restoration when an estimated 2,000+ people came to Aylestone Park. All day there were queues for the trip boats travelling the canal. The steam vehicles and vintage cars on show were much admired and the sales stand did a roaring trade in goods and raffle tickets.

The Mayor of Hereford, the late Councillor Julie Woodward, attended on the Sunday morning and "opened" the new stretch of canal cutting a ribbon across the slipway. She had to leave for another engagement at lunchtime - only to promptly return in the afternoon!

Figure 19: The Mayor of Hereford draws the winning raffle tickets (Author)

Four Wilderness Boats were moored in the park for the weekend, stopping off on the way to the IWA National Trail-boat Rally on the Neath Canal the following weekend.

Other boats, including a steam boat were launched from the new slipway. It was a remarkable day, the first canal event in the City's history.

The event was designed to be for all the family and featured a number of vintage vehicles including a steam roller and a rare steam lorry.

Figure 20: Steam vehicles at the Aylestone Park Boat Gathering (Author)

Restoration in Herefordshire

Despite the Canal Society and Trust promoting the canal for nearly 30 years, there were still people who said they never knew there was ever a canal in Hereford! Many more knew that there once was a canal, but had never expected to see boats on it again!

Figure 21: Trip boats in operation at Aylestone Park (Author)

Figure 22: Queuing for the trip boat in Aylestone Park (Author)

Restoration in Herefordshire

Figure 23: Wilderness trailable boats at Aylestone Park

In 2013 contractors began work on building a large overflow weir in the park which would not only manage the water level in the Hereford pound of the canal but is crucial to the management of surface water in parts of the City, some of which will be drained by the restored canal.

Figure 24: The foundations of the major overflow weir in Aylestone Park (Colin Dymott)

Restoration in Herefordshire

Figure 25: The overflow weir under construction in 2013 (Colin Dymott)

Now complete and landscaped, the weir itself is almost invisible from the park.

Adjacent to the partly restored canal in Aylestone Park is a length of canal beside the Holmer Trading Estate which, in 2009, was the subject of a planning application proposing a mixed development for residential, employment and retail purposes. The application was rejected on the grounds that it conflicted with the Council's planning policy to retain existing employment land unless there were benefits to outweigh it.

On appeal this decision was overturned, the Planning Inspector concluding:

Restoration of the length of canal indicated in the obligation would add substantially to the significance of the canal as a feature within the city. In my judgement, the benefit of the scheme to the restoration of the canal is sufficient to tip the balance in favour of allowing the appeal, notwithstanding the conflict with the provisions of UDP Policy E5

Herefordshire Council Appeal Decision APP/W1850/A/09/2098857

Clearly the appeal would have not been allowed if the proposal had not included the restoration of the canal. An agreement was reached which would transfer ownership of both the restored canal and the adjacent Aylestone Tunnel to the Trust. Construction work on this proposal was not begun but the planning application was successfully renewed.

In March 2015 Codex Land PCC Cell B successfully applied for outline Planning Permission to build 120 homes on the site but subsequently claimed that the cost of restoring the canal would not be viable to the building project and offered to safeguard the canal corridor at a cost of £160,000 - just to infill the canal and provide landscaping. The independent district valuer agreed.

The Council's Planning Committee, meeting in March 2018, felt its hands were tied and saw a danger that the site might remain derelict for many years if it refused this variation. It voted by twelve to two in favour of the new arrangements. This was a great blow to the Trust's ambitions to reach the City Centre, which is only about 1,000 metres from the end of Aylestone Tunnel. It has asked that ownership of the protected canal corridor be transferred to the Trust, but at the time of writing (2023) this has not happened.

The failure of the Holmer scheme is all the more disappointing since provision for the canal into the City Centre had already been partly provided as part of the development of the retail park on the site of the former Farriery College. This included a new road bridge and a substantial footbridge over the route of the canal which had already been built under a Section 106 Planning Agreement. This has more significance than it first appears as the crossings have been provided, not over the original line on which houses were built in the last century, but on an approved diversion. This creates an important precedent for the Trust, establishing the same protection for diversions as for the original line.

Work within Hereford City is now limited to maintenance of the canal in Aylestone Park, but it is hoped that the turn of events at Holmer will be no more than a temporary setback

The experience of other canal restoration groups teaches us that such disappointments should not be unexpected, especially in more urban areas where the changing plans and priorities of others do not always coincide with well-established restoration plans. It is therefore important that the primary vision is not lost and new opportunities found to deliver it in equally unforeseen ways.

Restoration in Herefordshire

Figure 26: The new Farriers Way road bridge in Hereford

Restoration in Gloucestershire

The work begun at Oxenhall by the Canal Society continued under the Trust. After the area around House Lock had been cleared, attention turned to the stretch of the canal towards Oxenhall Tunnel. The towpath under Cold Harbour Bridge was reinstated and some minor work carried out to restore the bridge itself.

This is one of only two remaining canal bridges surviving between Gloucester and Ledbury, the others having been demolished or replaced by railway bridges after 1881.

Figure 1: Cold Harbour Bridge before excavating the canal (Mike Potts)

The canal was then cleared and dredged up to the tunnel mouth with many tons of silt being removed. Only after this had been done was the true nature of the cutting revealed – it was hewn out of solid rock. The southern portal of the tunnel was also restored.

The excavation of the cutting in 1996 proved extremely difficult. Water was constantly flowing out of the tunnel and from streams in the side of the cutting. Several dumpers and the excavator were working in semi-liquid mud and on more than one occasion drivers had to be rescued from their equipment after becoming hopelessly stuck.

Restoration in Gloucestershire

Figure 2: The Oxenhall team discuss how best to free the excavator stuck in the mud (Mike Potts)

On the side of the towpath a brick structure was unearthed, the true nature of which may never be fully established. Known by the work parties as the "leggers rest" it may have been a refuge used by the professional leggers while waiting for boats to work through the tunnel.

There were clear signs of an "upper floor" which gave rise to suggestions that this might have been a stable with a hayloft above. Certainly, it is an unusual structure, the like of which I have never seen on British canals.

Figure 3: The leggers rest at Oxenhall (Mike Potts)

It made a good party venue for the Oxenhall Team.

131

Restoration in Gloucestershire

Figure 4: Party time in the leggers rest for the Oxenhall volunteers (Mike Potts)

Figure 5: The south portal of Oxenhall tunnel before restoration of the cutting (Mike Potts)

Figure 6: The approach to Oxenhall Tunnel from the South. Sadly, the channel has now completely silted up again (Mike Potts)

Eventually the whole length between Cold Harbour Bridge and the tunnel was cleared but it proved impossible at the time to prevent the channel rapidly silting up again.

Restoration in Gloucestershire

At present there is no agreement with landowners to enable further work to be carried out, which eventually will involve the building of silt traps on land adjoining the canal to prevent further silting.

Work was also carried out dredging the canal between Cold Harbour Bridge and Winter's Lane at the site of Top Lock. Lack of boat movement along this stretch has resulted in much weed growth but the towpath provides a pleasant walk.

Meanwhile, House Lock and the adjacent lock cottage were in a poor and deteriorating condition, with the unoccupied cottage suffering from repeated vandalism. Both were listed structures, so the Forest of Dean District Council issued several repair notices in the 1990s but the owner, Robin Stiles, was facing a constant battle with vandals and was unable to meet the requirements. It was judged that the value of the site, consisting of the cottage, House Lock and the line of the canal to beyond Ell Brook Aqueduct, was less than the commercial cost of repairs.

The Council threatened an Urgent Works Notice, but to avert this an agreement was reached such that the entire site was transferred to the Trust, with the proviso that when the cottage was sold, 10% of the value would go to Mr. Stiles. Thanks to his generosity, this therefore became the first piece of land to be owned by the Trust.

The removal of a garage adjacent to the lock cottage revealed the remains of a circular spill-weir, the outflow being culverted underneath the cottage to emerge below the lock. The spill-weir was painstakingly restored and used to divert water round the lock itself on which restoration was about to begin.

Figure 7: The remains of the spill weir
(Mike Potts)

When the first working party began work, the lock was hidden under dense undergrowth and little stonework was visible. Being a listed structure, it was necessary to restore the lock, as far as possible, to its condition at the time the canal was closed. After making what remained of the structure safe to work in, a small team of volunteers, working one day a week, began cutting and dressing stone, removing the existing unstable masonry and learning the craft of the mason as they did so.

Restoration in Gloucestershire

Figure 8: The restored Spill Weir in 2004 blending well into its surroundings (Author)

Figure 9: House Lock cleared of vegetation, ready for rebuilding start (Mike Potts)

While there was plenty of stonework remaining, much of it was in poor condition and could not be reused. Most conveniently, what remained of a nearby bridge from the Ledbury-Gloucester Railway was bought from British Railways for a nominal sum. When some of the stone blocks from this bridge were dressed for reuse they were found to be curiously recessed on their

Restoration in Gloucestershire

reverse side. These were quickly recognised as quoin-stones, presumably from one of the locks in the Oxenhall flight which had been demolished at the time of the building of the railway. They have now been returned to the canal!

The restoration involved the first substantial use of lime mortar by the Trust's volunteers, who also designed and installed special stainless-steel ties to secure the new stonework to the sound original inner structure of the lock chamber walls.

More stone was needed. Fortunately, a redundant railway bridge in Herefordshire was being demolished as part of the improvements to Roman Road, and several lorry-loads of stone were donated to the Trust and delivered to the site. By June 2004 the stonework had been completed and a formal ceremony was held at the lock-side to mark the achievement.

Figure 10: Marking the completion of the rebuilding of the stonework of House lock (Sallie Hopper)

As the actual use of the lock was inevitably some years off, gates and paddle gear were not installed. A footbridge, was however, erected over the tail of the lock. This was constructed of timbers from the Over Isolation Hospital which was being demolished at the time and which will feature again later in our story.

The cottage was sold to a new owner who under-took to repair it in accordance with the listed building requirements once the head of the lock and the spill-weir had been completed. As a canal side property, the sale included a provision for an annual index-linked payment to the Trust, setting a precedent which has been followed with all subsequent canal side developments. The sale proceeds provided funding to complete restoration of the lock itself.

Restoration in Gloucestershire

Figure 12: The fake plaque above the door of the lock cottage (Mike Potts)

Figure 11: The rebuilt chamber of House Lock, Oxenhall (Author)

Around this time a fake plaque mysteriously appeared above the door of the lock cottage. The name is wrong but the date is about right and from the ground it looked quite impressive, but upon closer inspection was discovered to be made of cardboard. No one knows how it got there. The cottage now bears one of the Trust's aluminium cast plaques.

Once the masonry of the lock was completed the Oxenhall team turned its attentions to the single-arched aqueduct which carried the canal over the Ell Brook, some 350 yards from the lock.

This is the largest surviving aqueduct on the canal and is of a rather strange design, being unusually wide. It appears that the canal may even have crossed it at an angle. It had fallen into a serious state of disrepair and threatened to collapse entirely into the brook below.

While the Oxenhall group had acquired considerable skill in preparing and laying masonry in rebuilding the lock, the construction of a stone aqueduct was quite a different matter and very much less straightforward.

The first task was to stabilise the arch itself and fortunately within the group there were skills to design and construct a steel support to prevent further movement and allow the work to proceed safely. This also acted as a former to enable the new masonry to be laid on the correct alignment. The

Restoration in Gloucestershire

spandrel walls were then reconstructed using stone from a variety of sources, most of the original stone being unusable.

Figure 13: The Ell Brook aqueduct in a sorry state of repair (Mike Potts)

Figure 14: Restoration of the Ell Brook aqueduct. Constructing the steel former supporting the arch.
(Geoff Hopper)

Restoration in Gloucestershire

During the summer months the Ell Brook is a placid stream, with perhaps six inches depth of water, but after heavy rain the level can rise dramatically to within inches of the top of the arch. Work on more than one occasion had to be suspended because of these conditions as the site was inundated with rocks and silt being carried downstream. The rebuilding of the aqueduct took the small Oxenhall group four years to complete. The canal has not yet been reinstated over the aqueduct because changes to the canal level may be required elsewhere and the precise level at this point has yet to be determined.

Figure 15: The rebuilt Ell Brook aqueduct (Author)

Adjacent to the site of the Ell Brook aqueduct is a large area of land through which the canal originally ran before passing under the B4215, Newent to Dymock Road. Previously occupied by the Willows Nursery, this had been compulsorily purchased by the Highways Agency to enable improvements to the local roads to be made but these plans were subsequently scrapped and the land was no longer required. In 2000 the Agency announced that the land was to be auctioned as a whole – far beyond what the Trust could realistically bid. The Trust had been unable to persuade the Agency to split the site and to sell the land formerly occupied by the canal to the Trust for a nominal sum, as had been the case with British Rail at another small site adjacent to the Ell Brook restoration site.

The auction was announced for July 7th just ten days after the Deputy Prime Minister, John Prescott, launched "Waterways for Tomorrow" which required both local and national government departments to recognise the value of our waterways and to support restoration projects by, among other means, not allowing developments to take place which could impede future schemes.

Armed with an obscure government circular identified by the Trust covering the interpretation of "best value" in sales of land, the MP for the Forest of Dean, Diana Organ, swung into immediate action and demanded that the sale be postponed. At 3.30pm John Prescott cancelled the auction just three hours before it was due to take place, no doubt much to the astonishment and disappointment of a number of potential bidders. Smith's, the auctioneers, were equally surprised. John Parrott, of Smiths, said he has never come across a situation like this before.

"It was a real shock," he said. "We had an inclination (sic) that there was a bit of bother over it but then, at 3.30pm, the Highways Agency cancelled it. It was pretty tough because there were a lot of people geared up to buy it."

While the immediate danger from the auction was averted, the matter was far from resolved as the Highways Agency still took the view that it was obliged to obtain the best value it could for the land it held.

From the outset the Trust had argued that, under the Local Government Act 1972 General Disposal Consents (1998), "best value" was not limited to financial return but could include the value of benefits to the local community and the environment. Important though the Newent site was to the Trust, there were implications for restoration schemes across the country. It was vital that the argument was resolved in the Trust's favour.

Diana Organ continued her battle in Parliament and Whitehall and in May 2002 succeeded in arranging a meeting of two of the Trust Directors, supported by the Chief Executive of the Waterways Trust, with the then Transport Minister, David Jamieson MP. The Trust went to the Palace of Westminster well prepared. The case that the long-term benefits which the restored canal would bring to the area must far outweigh the short-term financial gain to the Agency was strongly argued.

A letter was produced from the Forest of Dean District Council confirming that it would be prepared to use its powers of compulsory purchase, if necessary, to enable restoration to take place – so why sell to a third party only to have it compulsorily purchased later? The Minister expressed surprise that land could be so acquired for canal restoration – and was even more astonished to learn that the Waterways Trust had facilitated the compulsory purchase of part of a Sainsbury's store for the Huddersfield Narrow Canal!

The meeting, however, was a positive one and it was clear that the Minister was sympathetic and would do what he could to help. A formal, lengthy, submission was made by the Trust. This resulted in the land being offered to the Trust, but as another party had already offered some £20,000 for the land, that was the sum demanded. The Trust rejected this and went back to the Minister to argue for a further change to Government policy such that not only would any land in public ownership on the line of the canal have to be made available for restoration but it would also have to be offered at nominal value – a most crucial rider. This was accepted and in September 2003 the Highways Agency offered all of the land to the Trust for an agreed nominal sum of £1,000, or some £600 per acre.

It had been a long battle, but a vital victory had been won to the benefit, not only of the Trust, but of all other canal restorations.

Restoration of the canal through The Willows site has still to be commenced. The original line of the canal passed below what is now the B4215 Newent-Dymock road but that was lowered to allow the railway to pass above it. Any crossing would require significant changes to the level of the canal and it is now planned to carry the canal through the Willows site and to pass over the B4215, using the old railway abutments. More than one scheme has been proposed to achieve this but final plans have still to be developed.

In the meantime, nine miles away in Gloucester, the Trust had for several years also been addressing quite different concerns. The canal's connection with the River Severn by means of Over Lock was situated on land owned by the West Midlands Regional Health Authority, having been the site of Over Isolation Hospital which closed in 1992. The following year the Authority began the process of disposing of the buildings and the large site they occupied. At the first meeting of the Secretary of State's advisers with Tewkesbury Borough Council, the Council made it clear that proposals would not be considered unless provision for the canal restoration was included. The Council had agreed to the protection of the line of the canal only the previous year. Various proposals were made, including an offenders' rehabilitation centre and a supermarket, but both were overtaken by changes in Council planning policy.

Eventually a plan for a residential development of 44 houses was proposed, but this was then amended to 33 before submission to the Council. The Trust lodged a technical objection to these proposals to ensure it had a place at the Inquiry where it could negotiate the gain for the canal. The Trust saw this as an opportunity to work closely with both any potential developer and he Council to prepare a scheme which brought mutual benefit. Under the leadership of one of the Trust's Directors, revised plans were drawn up around the concept of a development which made a feature of the canal and its junction basin around which the proposed housing would be focused.

At the Inquiry in December 1997 the Trust obtained an adjournment in order to draw up a Section 106 agreement which had long been promised by the Department of Health, but had not materialised. A tight deadline for early January 1998 was imposed by the planning inspector, otherwise he was "minded to grant planning permission without it". This meant the frantic preparation over Christmas and New Year of the Trust's proposals, including gaining approval from both Tewkesbury Borough Council and the Secretary of State for Health.

The case was made and the Inquiry then found in favour of the Trust. In essence this required the developer, whoever that might be, to transfer to the Trust the ownership of the land occupied by the canal, the basin and lock, together with the lock cottage which had first to be made safe and weather-tight. The developer was also required to accept the soil excavated from the canal and contribute a significant sum of money to fund the Trust's work which would be carried out by volunteers.

For its part, the Trust was required to excavate the line of the canal and the basin, build a new wharf wall 75 metres long, and make arrangements for water to be abstracted from the River Leadon to maintain the water level of the basin. It also had to provide a surfaced towpath. But there was a sting in the tail of this agreement – the Trust's work had to be completed by September 2000 when it was expected the first houses would be ready for sale.

Figure 16: Over Hospital site in 1998. The building seen is the Mortuary Block (Nigel Bailey)

Restoration in Gloucestershire

Early in 1998, before the start of the nesting season, all of the trees which had become established on the line of the canal and surrounding areas were removed. In the summer the site was cleared of scrub in preparation for the excavation of the canal and basin.

Figure 17: The start of excavation in 1998 (Nigel Bailey)

Figure 18: The first concrete pour for the wharf wall foundation (Cliff Penny)

Restoration in Gloucestershire

In the space of nine days a small team of volunteers using a large hired excavator and dumpers carrying 25 tons of soil at a time made an impressive start to the excavation. Some of the spoil was used to infill the site of the old mill pond, the rest for landscaping and to build noise bunds to reduce the sound of the traffic on the adjacent A40 trunk road.

By the Spring of 1999 a Waterway Recovery Group work camp had completed that part of the task and the task of building the wharf wall could begin. Three of the twelve pours of concrete for the foundations of the wall were completed by the start of the summer.

The project plan had assumed that the bricks for the wharf wall would be recycled from the parts of the hospital which were to be demolished, but by May 1999 demolition had not begun. A WRG training weekend had been arranged and it been expected that bricks would be available for this so a start could be made on the brickwork of the wharf wall. The Trust said it would take the building down itself if the bricks did not arrive in time, a comment the developer did not take seriously until the Trust did precisely that. A single storey part of one of the wards was carefully demolished to provide a supply of bricks to be sorted and cleaned ready for the weekend.

Figure 19: Recycling bricks and other material from the 1903 block of Over Hospital (Nigel Bailey)

As the demolition contractors' work got under way a ready supply of bricks became available for cleaning for reuse. Anything else of possible value was also salvaged – doors, skirtings, architraves and nearly 8,000 wood floor blocks. All the materials were cleaned and carefully stored, a major and often tedious task.

Restoration in Gloucestershire

During the rest of 1999 local volunteers and a number of WRG camps saw the construction of the two brick wharf walls and the slipway. At the WRG Reunion Weekend about 140 volunteers were divided into teams working on different parts of the site. Work continued unabated with further WRG camps and long hours of local volunteer labour.

Figure 20: The slipway under construction at Over basin (Cliff Penny)

Figure 21: The newly filled canal basin in 2000 (Nigel Bailey)

Restoration in Gloucestershire

In early August 2000, as the deadline for completion approached, the last of the bricks of the wharf walls were laid and on Thursday August 10th the pump lent to the Trust by Sterling Fluid Systems began to lift water from the River Leadon to feed the basin and canal. By the following Wednesday both were full.

For two years this had been the largest all-volunteer waterway restoration project in the country. Following years of frustrating negotiations, a large area of scrubby, untidy land had been transformed into an attractive landscaped canal basin entirely by volunteers and at a tenth of the cost which would have been incurred had contractors been used.

On September 29th 2000 Timothy West and Prunella Scales performed the opening ceremony, unveiling plaques on the feature wall beside the basin.

This wall, built, like almost everything else, of recycled bricks, has the letters "H&G" and "WRG" picked out in blue bricks, a permanent reminder of the partnership which delivered the restored basin on time and on budget.

Figure 22: The formal opening Over Basin by Timothy West and Prunella Scales in September 2000 (Nigel Bailey)

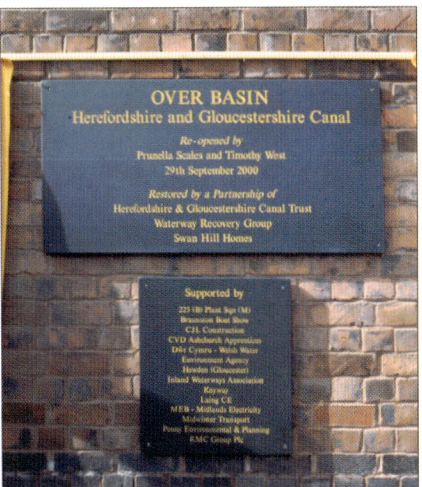

Notwithstanding the huge efforts of the Trust's volunteers, it was the support from the Waterway Recovery Group which made the task possible in the time allowed.

Part of the opening ceremony was filmed by Central TV as part of their Water World series. The Trust's small trip boat, Mister Maysey, began the event by carrying the VIPs across the basin.

Figure 23: The plaque commemorating the opening of Over Basin (Nigel Bailey)

Restoration in Gloucestershire

The cabin was filled with local dignitaries, much weighed down with mayoral chains of office. The skipper, your author, watched in horror as the boat dropped lower and lower in the water. The petrol tank, which normally sat at the stern well above water level now bobbed alarmingly around.

Mr. West and Miss Scales then boarded and stood on the stern deck ready to be interviewed as we cruised across the basin, so we were joined by the film crew – cameraman, sound recordist and director together with all the accoutrements required for modern TV recording.

With almost zero freeboard – the height between the water level and the lowest point water can enter a boat - Mister Maysey set out across the basin – a journey of only fifty yards or so. To the skipper, watching for the first signs of the boat actually sinking, the trip seemed interminable, while everyone else on board were quite oblivious of the very real danger of the whole party having to swim for the shore.

While this would have made sensational television, it was with great relief that the wharf was reached, the boat secured to the mooring rings and the passengers disembarked onto dry land.

Figure 24: 'Mister Maysey' in serious danger of sinking during recording an episode of ITV's Water World.

In 2001 work started on another major but largely invisible project, the building of the pump shaft, silt trap and abstraction and feeder channels to allow for the canal to be permanently filled. Three 2.5 metre diameter pipes, surplus to a long sea outfall project in Cardiff, were set on end to form the 9-metre-deep pump shaft. Underground ducting was installed to carry services to the wharf, where the outlets are housed in "dog kennels" and to the pump house. The car park for the basin and The Wharf House was also built, carefully landscaped to intrude as little as possible into the site.

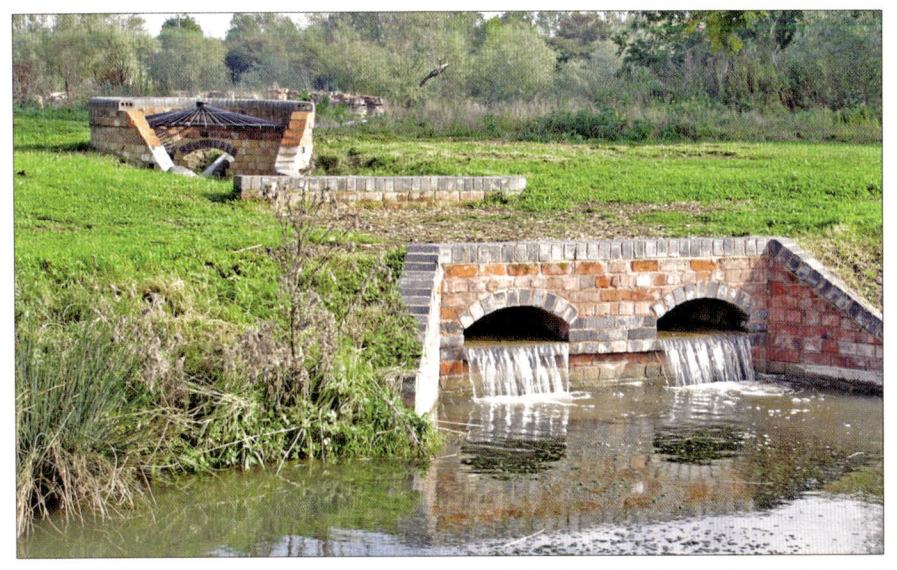

Figure 25: The new water supply for Over Basin in operation (Ted Beagles)

Seen from Over Basin, the canal shortly disappears round a left-hand bend, but walking the towpath quickly brought one to the end of the restored canal – still a very long way from Hereford! The next length of the canal passed through a piece of land bought in 2004 by a consortium of 28 residents of Staunton's Hill, the development occupying the rest of the Over Hospital site. In 2011 negotiations with the owners resulted in the sale of the line of the canal to the Trust, potentially allowing the length of the canal at Over to be more than doubled. A condition of the sale was that restoration work had to be completed within 12 months, by September 2012.

On September 3rd 2011 two longstanding volunteers at Over ceremoniously cut through the wire fence separating the new site from the old and work on site clearance began.

With a new project came new volunteers. During the first few weeks, 26 different people turned up to help, ten of whom had not worked at Over before. All the scrub and trees which had to be removed had gone long before the nesting season began and the top soil had been stripped from the canal line. At one point a major failure of an excavator engine brought work to a temporary halt. Despite being stuck in the middle of the site 150 yards from the end of the towpath, the engine was winched out, the accessory parts transferred to a new engine before this was winched in and installed into the machine. Only four working days were lost.

Figure 26: Site clearance at Vineyard Hill in September 2011 (Ted Beagles)

Figure 27: Start of excavation at Vineyard Hill (Ted Beagles)

Restoration in Gloucestershire

During the first two weeks of April 2012 members of the Waterway Recovery Group assisted in carrying out the actual excavation of the canal. On April 15th the dam between the existing canal and the newly excavated stretch was lowered slightly, the pump lifting water from the River Leadon was started and water flowed from the old to the new length.

Three hours later the first pair of ducks arrived on the new stretch of canal.

Although five months ahead of schedule, there was still much to be done finishing the towpath and landscaping the rest of the site. Progress towards this was interrupted by an unexpected rise in the water level caused by persistent rainfall in the spring and early summer. The canal bank was raised to prevent damage by water overflowing onto the towpath.

The first boat, albeit of the rowing variety, navigated the canal from the slipway to a winding hole at the far end of the new length and back on May 2nd.

By July the dam between the two lengths was removed and the Trust's ex-British Waterways tug Alder navigated from the basin to the new winding hole.

After further tidying the site was ready for its official opening as part of the Over Canal Festival on September 1st and 2nd. Prunella Scales and Timothy West returned to Over to unveil a plaque to mark the occasion. Once again a restored length of canal had been completed on time entirely by volunteers.

Figure 28: The newly restored Vineyard Hill section in September 2012 (Ted Beagles)

149

Restoration in Gloucestershire

On September 1st 2012 Jason Pullen, Managing Director of Gloucester Quays, on the bow of Mister Maysey, officially cut the ribbon to open the new Vineyard Hill section.

Figure 29: The ribbon is cut, opening the new canal at Vineyard Hill (Cliff Penny)

Earlier the same year the Trust had reached agreement with the owners of Moat Farm at Malswick some five and a half miles from Gloucester. Although this part of the canal was largely obliterated by the railway, the latter took a more direct route at this point leaving a stretch of canal very much overgrown by trees and scrub but normally retaining a reasonable depth of water.

Steady progress has been made in clearing the site ready for future excavation when the water has been drained. The site extends to some 600 yards with about 100 yards at each end over which the railway line passed.

Some of the railway embankment at the Gloucester end of the site has been removed and the canal bed and towpath reinstated. Just beyond this length is the site of the bottom lock of the staircase which caused so much trouble for Howard Williams and his friends in 1875.

Excavation of the canal in the southern part of the site commenced in the Spring of 2014. A section of the offside bank had been removed when the railway line was constructed in the early 1880's and this had to be reinstated. It was also necessary to avoid disturbing the existing puddle clay and trial excavations were carried out in order to establish its position and depth. This

Restoration in Gloucestershire

process was assisted by the finding of freshwater mussel shells. The mussels would have lived in the layer of accumulated silt above the clay so indicating the depth of excavation required. By the autumn the excavated canal was filling with water naturally, the puddle clay clearly doing its job.

Figure 30: Part of the Moat Farm site in 2012

Figure 31: A section of the canal at Moat Farm still holding water after 200 years of neglect

151

Restoration in Gloucestershire

Figure 32: The line of the canal can clearly be seen from the old railway bridge where the line has diverged from the canal.

The railway line followed a gradient of 1 in 230 along the Moat Farm site resulting in the track bed being some eight feet higher at the northern end of the site than at the south end. As the canal is level along this length the amount of material to be excavated increases considerably until it reaches the end of the site where the Double Locks raised the water level by over 18ft.

Figure 33: The old railway bridge provides useful cover for the restoration team and their materials.

Restoration in Gloucestershire

Figure 34: The canal at Moat Farm in the Autumn of 2014 (Wilf Jones)

Restoration in Gloucestershire

Figure 35: The maturing canal at Moat Farm in January 2023

Work on the middle and northern sections of the site were carried out during 2015 and 2018 working towards the site of the Double Locks.

Having completed much of the restoration work required at Moat Farm, maintenance resources were largely transferred to a demanding new undertaking nearby.

A major project at Malswick was launched in 2017 involving a length of canal less than a mile from the Double Locks at the northern end of the Moat Farm site. Following negotiations with the landowners, the Gloucester Charities Trust and their tenants Hartpury College, it was agreed that the Canal Trust would restore two existing brick bridges over the Ell Brook which runs nearby, and construct a new bridge 16ft wide and capable of carrying 32 tons.

In return, the ownership of approximately ¾ mile of the canal line running alongside the B4215 Newent-Gloucester road would be transferred to the Trust. The work on the two existing bridges would include the removal of excess vegetation on the banks of the brook, repairing the foundations and a complete rebuild of the parapets and wing walls.

The landscaping would also include the construction of about 650 metres of boundary fencing and two new field fences. The canal passes through two areas of woodland giving the opportunity to create new wildlife corridors alongside the route.

154

Restoration in Gloucestershire

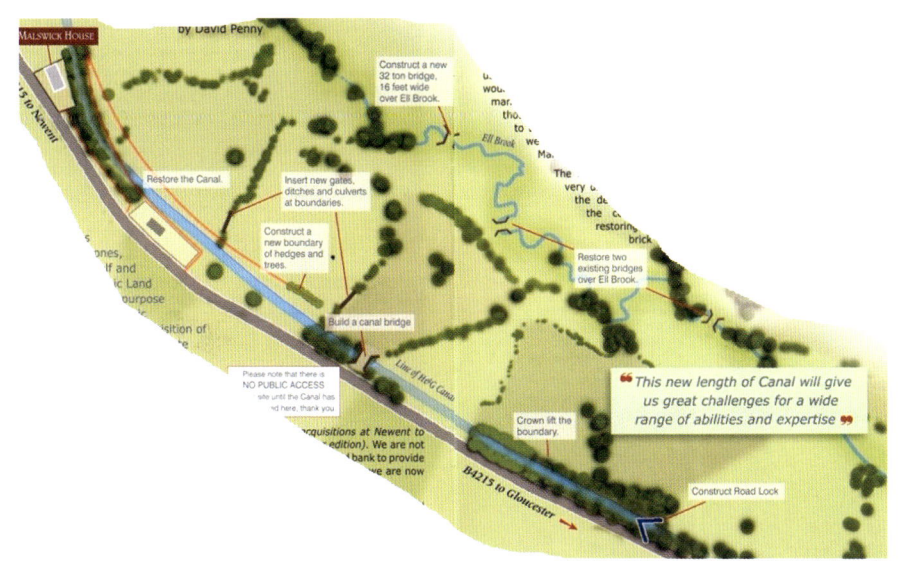

Figure 36: Malswick project site

Figure 37: The locals reluctant to have their peace disturbed (Paul Henshaw)

Once the agreement had been reached two volunteer teams were tasked to work on the two brick bridges, one from the Oxenhall site and the other from Moat Farm, and by the autumn of 2017 work was progressing rapidly. These old bridges were attractive, vernacular structures and the repairs were carried out to preserve the original appearance as far as possible.

Restoration in Gloucestershire

Figure 38: Malswick east Bridge after initial work prior to restoration (Paul Henshaw)

Figure 39: Less than comfortable working conditions while carrying out repairs to the underside of the east bridge (Paul Henshaw)

Work progressed rapidly and by October attention was turned to the repairs and the necessity to erect scaffolding over the Brook. A local building company offered the services of one of their professional scaffolders who erected the scaffolding at both bridges and provided training for our volunteers. This was

Restoration in Gloucestershire

offered free of charge thus saving the Trust a very considerable expense. The scaffolding provided a safe working platform above the Brook to enable the best quality of work on the outside of the parapet walls. Inevitably, as winter set in the Ell Brook flooded and work transferred to clearing the small west woodland area, through which the canal and railway line ran.

Figure 40: Scaffold Training at Malswick (Alan McBride)

Figure 41: The Malswick volunteers demonstrating their faith in their scaffolding skills.

Restoration in Gloucestershire

Figure 42: The west bridge parapet nearing completion (Paul Henshaw)

Figure 43: The completed east bridge merging into its surroundings (Geoff Hopper)

By the early summer of 2018 both the east and west bridges were completed. Once the brickwork has weathered, a casual observer might wonder what all the fuss has been about, since the bridges will look as though they have stood here for years. That, of course, was precisely the intention.

The third bridge, however, had to carry a weight of 32 tons so would require a quite different approach.

Restoration in Gloucestershire

In May the necessary consents were given allowing work to commence.

The new bridge had been designed with the help of Tony Gee & Partners and took the form of a steel beam structure with a concrete deck.

Over the rest of 2018 priority was given to the construction of the new bridge. In June piling contractors sank six piles on either side the bridge to a depth of between six and seven metres. During August the first of the two concrete pours took place to create the base for the 18 steel beams which would carry the bridge deck across the brook. The second was completed in September and the beams craned into place.

Figure 44: Preparing one of the abutments of the bridge. (Paul Henshaw)

Work continued apace and by the Autumn the deck plates were welded to the beams. In early October concrete was poured simultaneously from both sides of the bridge to ensure an equal loading across the bridge structure.

Figure 45: Pile cap with rubber bearing mat. (Paul Henshaw)

159

Restoration in Gloucestershire

Figure 46: Synchronised concrete pour. (Paul Henshaw)

Figure 47: Bridge sides on, ready for decking. (Paul Henshaw)

Figure 48: Gabions filled with crushed concrete were installed at either side of the approach ramps to protect the ramps when the brook floods. (Geoff Hopper)

Restoration in Gloucestershire

Figure 49: The completed new bridge at Malswick capable of bearing loads of up to 32 tons
(Ralph Ward)

Figure 50: The completed new bridge at Malswick (Ralph Ward)

With the bridge complete, the team moved to a site behind Malswick House, the pub owned by the Trust. Once again, this was work undertaken for the Gloucester Charities Trust consisting of a new culvert to carry a stream under a trackway in exchange for a further stretch of the canal behind the pub.

Restoration in Gloucestershire

Figure 51: The headwall of the new culvert at Malswick (Alan McBride)

After enlarging the stream ditch three 1.2 metre concrete pipes were laid, kindly donated by Complete Utilities Ltd. using a 13-ton digger provided by the Keyway Group. Crushed concrete backfill was then dropped either side of the pipes and 40 tons more placed to form the bed of the culvert, topped with railway ballast reclaimed from the west woodland. The headwalls of the culvert were built up using a dry concrete mix in hessian bags.

The Malswick Team spent 2019 and the early part of 2020 preparing the ground for the excavation of the new length of canal, but in the Spring of 2020 the Covid-19 pandemic brought site work to a halt.

The time was not wasted, however, as much work had to be done to prepare a Planning Application for the 600 metres of canal. The initial application was withdrawn on the advice of the Trust's consultants and resubmitted in April 2021. It was granted consent the following November.

The following months were spent preparing the route of the canal in advance of a major summer camp in June and July when our own volunteers would be assisted by the Kent and East Sussex section of the Waterway Recovery Group. The canal route is crossed by two streams which needed to be diverted through culverts for the canal to pass over them, the larger requiring a two-metre diamenter pipe which was lowered into place on June 21st. With the block work forming the chambers and end walls of the culverts complete, the pipes were bedded in with gravel topped with soil.

162

Restoration in Gloucestershire

Figure 52: The first of the pipes forming the large culvert is lowered into place (Mark Atkin)

Figure 53: WRG and HGCT Volunteers and heavy plant ready for action at Malswick (Mark Atkin)

Excavation of the canal itself has now begun. A good start has been made, with plans to complete the excavation in 2023.

Restoration in Gloucestershire

Figure 54: Modern heavy plant accomplishes in hours what large teams of navvies in the 19th century achieved in days or weeks with picks, shovels and wheelbarrows (Mark Atkin)

Llanthony Lock

The canal's connection to the River Severn at Over and thence to the rest of the waterway network has been something of a challenge since its very earliest days. Entry into the deep lock at Over from the tidal river required some very skillful manoeuvring on the part of the boatmen and while help was given, there were a number of serious accidents and sinking of boats.

Navigation on the river may have become a little easier for the last 10 years of the canal's working life when Maisemore and Llanthony locks were built on the river. Maisemore Lock and its cottage were sold by British Waterways in the 1980s before restoration of the canal it served was imagined, but Llanthony Lock, though partly infilled, remained in the possession of British Waterways until 2008.

Although not, of course, part of the Hereford and Gloucester Canal, after lengthy negotiations the lock was bought by the Canal Trust for £150,000, together with the pair of lock cottages, a considerable area of surrounding land and a stretch of the River Severn including both banks and Llanthony Weir. Very significantly, the agreement also gave the Trust control of both Maisemore and Llanthony weirs but without liability for them. The purchase was made possible through a legacy from Miss Beth Gaddesden.

Restoration of Llanthony lock would enable access from the Severn from below Over Lock giving a much easier upstream approach than would have been made downstream from Maisemore. The latter would have involved a turn just before the railway bridge, the central piers of which would constitute a significant navigational hazard.

A project team was set up to carry out a programme of work to prevent further deterioration of the site and the cottages, and the first steps towards restoration of the lock. The team would have a wide range of work to do, from major site clearance and continuing maintenance to general repairs to the cottages. The first immediate challenge was to begin to deal with the growth of Japanese knotweed which had begun to invade the site, the start of a determined battle which would take some years before the weed was finally eradicated.

During the summer of 2009 a large site hut was erected on the site – no small feat as all the sections had to be carried on to the site over the footbridge. Unfortunately the roof sections were too large to fit under the cross-braces of

Llanthony Lock

the bridge and had to be carried a far longer way around. The next job was to provide a car park and toilet facilities.

Figure 1: Llanthony Lock in 2012

Having provided the basic infrastructure for work to be carried out on the site, attention was turned to the cottages where guttering was replaced and new fencing erected. Scrub clearance around the site continued, as did the long battle against the knotweed. The lock cut approach to the top of the lock was cleared.

In 2010 a team from the Waterway Recovery Group helped the local volunteers with several necessary tasks including the removal of an old footbridge over the lock and stump clearance in the downstream lock cut. Later in the year further fencing was erected, power and water supplies brought to the site hut from the cottages and new windows installed in the cottages themselves.

The following year further work improving the cottages was carried out including renovation of the lock-keeper's office – ready for the first boats to arrive! The painstaking and tedious task of stripping years of old paint from the very decorative Victorian railings in front of the cottages prior to repainting was begun – and yet more fencing was erected!

A new floor was provided for cottage No.1 and further restoration carried out on both cottages. The pipe-box enclosing the water supply as it is carried over

Llanthony Lock

the Severn on the river footbridge was replaced without any volunteers having an unexpected swim, and other important landscaping work was carried out across the site. The cottages are now let, providing a reliable income stream for the Trust.

Figure 2: Llanthony Lock cottages (Ted Beagles)

Figure 3: Llanthony Lock cottages gardens (Ted Beagles)

Llanthony Lock

The main access to the cottages is via the footbridge over the river which the Trust acquired as part of the agreement with British Waterways. In addition to foot traffic and services to the cottages, the bridge also carries an important pipe forming part of the Government Pipeline and Storage System. Negotiation with the Government Pipeline Agency in 2012 led to a transfer of liability for maintenance of the footbridge, at no cost, from the Trust to the Agency.

While it was clear why the Trust had wanted to purchase Llanthony Lock, less obvious was why it should also want so much land around the lock, control of the weirs and a stretch of the Severn itself. In 2012 the 'hidden agenda' for the site was revealed.

The restoration of the lock was only part of the Trust's vision for the site. In December, Richard Benyon MP, the Environment Minister, chaired a meeting attended by senior officers from British Waterways (soon to become the Canal and River Trust), Gloucestershire and Herefordshire Councils, the Environment Agency and other interested parties. At this meeting the Trust's Commercial and Development Director launched Llanthony Hydro, a Hydro-Electric, Flood Relief and Lock scheme.

Under the proposals outlined, inflatable weirs at Llanthony and Maisemore would significantly increase control of the River Severn, both at normal river levels and in times of flood, and would prevent tidal flows with the accompanying debris above the weirs. This would greatly help navigation through the East Channel and the access to Gloucester Docks. It would also very significantly reduce the silting of the river, the docks and the Gloucester and Sharpness Canal as currently water carrying fine estuarine silt is pumped into the docks from just above the weir.

A new lock to replace the old Llanthony Lock would be fitted with radial gates which would enable the lock and lock cut to function as a flood relief channel. A major component of the scheme would include hydro-electricity generation to meet the long-term energy requirements of operating the canal – another example of the Trust's commitment to sustainability.

There are obvious advantages in this scheme far beyond those to the Trust. There is equally clearly an immense amount of planning to be done to develop the scheme to the point where contractors can begin the work. Because of the number of beneficiaries of the scheme, funding is potentially available from a variety of sources, but it will be some years before very much becomes visible at the site.

Llanthony Lock

The design, construction and operation of a modern tidal river lock is a very significant and expensive undertaking and one which the Trust could hardly dream of undertaking on its own. A partnership with players far bigger and stronger than itself, and with a wide range of additional benefits, makes the project not only achievable but a potential source of lasting income for the Trust rather than a drain on resources, but real progress lies outside the Trust's control.

At the time of writing there seems to have been little progress on the Llanthony Hydro scheme and in the shorter term the Trust may have to look at alternative options to achieve the canal's connection with the River Severn.

Figure 4: Llanthony lock, still operational in the 1950s (British Waterways)

169

Commercial and Environmental Sustainability

Commercial Sustainability

Most canals and rivers in England and Wales are owned and managed by the Canal and River Trust (CRT) which was formed in 2012 as successor to British Waterways. The CRT's income derives from a number of sources including utilities such as fibre-optic data cables and water sales, rental income from its property portfolio including marinas, and license and mooring fees from boaters. But the largest single component of its income is from a fixed grant from the Department for the Environment, Food and Rural Affairs (DEFRA).

At present the total income of the CRT is increasingly less than that required to improve, or even maintain, the 200 year old canal network. While the CRT is supportive of restoration schemes which will make more miles of navigable waterways available to the public, it is not expected to incorporate them into its own network unless it can be shown that they generate more income than their maintenance costs.

From the earliest days of the Herefordshire and Gloucestershire Canal Trust it was understood that the restored canal would have to pay its way. It must generate enough revenue to cover all its operational and maintenance costs. Income from mooring fees, and boat or angling licences will never be sufficient to provide sufficient income. It is unlikely to receive significant ongoing grant aid and most people who visit canals do so by foot or by bicycle and therefore pay nothing at all. It was also recognised that both financial and environmental sustainability needs to be developed as the canal is restored or rebuilt, not added as an afterthought.

This will be done by using the canal corridor, the land though which the canal and towpath passes, to its maximum potential. One of the key ways of doing this is to work with developers to incorporate long-term advantages to the Trust through the planning process. It had begun in a small way with the lock cottage at Oxenhall which required its future owners to make an index-linked payment to the Trust. A more significant income stream was developed in association with the restored basin at Over.

The Wharf House

The agreement with the developers of the Over Hospital site included an undertaking to stabilise and make weatherproof the former Lock Cottage in

Commercial and Environmental Sustainability

order for it then to be the converted by the Trust, perhaps to provide a Visitor Centre, shop and small tea-room. This cottage had been built by Stephen Ballard in 1831 to house the Over lock keeper. It originally had three rooms upstairs and two down with a back kitchen. It was later extended and named "The Lodge" and used by the hospital to house the Hospital Engineer. It was occupied until 1971, after which time the structure of the building deteriorated rapidly.

When daylight appeared between the original part of the house and the extension it became apparent that it was impractical to make the building safe at reasonable cost and the agreement was changed such that the cottage was demolished and a new building erected on the site.

Figure 1: The former lock cottage at Over (Mike Potts)

While the loss of any building associated with the canal was to be regretted, it was not an object of great beauty and had been considerably altered. Even if a sympathetic restoration had been possible, the building would have been a dubious asset of limited practical value to the Trust.

The new agreement provided for a building five times the size of the original cottage, on three floors, designed to complement the houses being built nearby while expressing the style of traditional canal architecture. The developer was required to deliver just the shell of the building, the only internal walls being those around the central staircase. The building, to be called "The Wharf House", was handed over from Swan Hill Homes to the Trust in November 2002.

The volunteers who had been working outdoors on the Over site now swung into action building walls, laying floors and fitting doors, skirtings, and ceilings. Plumbing and electrical systems were installed and gradually the rough shell of the building began to be transformed. As much as possible of the materials used were recycled from the old hospital which had been built to a high standard. Thousands of wooden floor blocks were cleaned and re-laid; skirtings, doors and architraves were stripped of paint and reused.

Commercial and Environmental Sustainability

Figure 2: The Wharf House in 2013 (The Wharf House)

In 2003 The Wharf House Company was established to oversee the fit-out and plan for the commercial use of the building. The ground floor was divided into a restaurant area and a spacious Visitor Centre and shop. Some professional help was necessary to deal with specialised work including the provision of a commercial kitchen.

Figure 3: The Wharf House restaurant (The Wharf House)

Commercial and Environmental Sustainability

After thousands of hours of volunteer effort supported by five-figure grants from the Heritage Lottery Fund, DEFRA, and the Gloucester Environmental Trust as well as generous donations from local businesses and supporters of the Trust, the ground floor was opened in 2005.

It had been a mammoth task – and now work could be concentrated on the two upper floors. Here there were to be six luxury bedrooms together with office and storage facilities. There followed five years of intense work, almost all of it by volunteers until, in 2010, there was an informal "private opening" for Trust members to celebrate the completion of this part of the task.

In 2012, a seventh bedroom was opened; this, being on the ground floor, is ideally suited for less-abled guests and for those with canine companions. The restaurant received the AA's Red Rosette for the excellence of the cuisine and four Gold Stars for the seven bedrooms.

Figure 4: One of the seven bedrooms in the Wharf House (The Wharf House)

The Wharf House also received an award from the Council for the Protection of Rural England in recognition of the contribution to the environment and to the local community which the creation of The Wharf House and the restoration of Over Canal Basin has made. The entire roof of the building is furnished with solar panels, 94 in all, which was the largest roof-mounted installation in Gloucestershire when it was completed and is a visible example of the Trust's commitment to environmental sustainability.

Commercial and Environmental Sustainability

The location of The Wharf House adjacent to the basin and, above the River Severn creates a splendid setting, and when a Severn Bore is due, a very dramatic one. The Waterside Restaurant became recognised as one of the highest quality restaurants in Gloucestershire and on summer evenings Tapas on the Terrace proved very popular. The setting was greatly enhanced by the landscaping and planting of the area round The Wharf House. Trees planted in the early days are now maturing well.

For ten years The Wharf House Company managed The Wharf House with a combination of employed staff and volunteers, but in 2019 the decision was made to hand over the day-to-day management of the business to a third party and the business was re-branded as The Lock Keepers.

Figure 5: The Wharf House Terrace (The Wharf House)

Back in September 2013 The Wharf House Company had purchased the freehold of The Traveller's Rest at Malswick, situated on the main Gloucester to Newent road. This was achieved in a remarkably short time as the auction was held only a week after the proposed sale of the property came to the notice of the Trust, the previous tenant having ceased trading less than a month before. Paperwork supporting a bid, including a financial analysis, was prepared and the Trust's Council of Management discussed this in a 1½ hour telephone conference involving all Council members, reaching a unanimous agreement to go ahead.

The principal reason why the Trust, through The Wharf House Company, was

Commercial and Environmental Sustainability

anxious to secure the freehold of the property is that it is the only remaining pub directly adjacent to the route of the canal in Gloucestershire, the line of the canal adjoining its rear garden. After initial renovation by Canal Trust volunteers and renaming as Malswick House, the pub opened for business in 2014, run by a tenant on a lease which included payment of a proportion of the turnover back to The Trust.

Figure 6: Malswick House (Maggie Jones)

However, the business failed to make a profit, not helped by a five-week closure of the B4215 in 2017, and for a period it was closed. Following the Covid 19 Pandemic it reopened in 2021 under new management and it is hoped that the future will be brighter, especially when restoration work on the adjacent canal brings a navigable section of the canal to its back door.

Ecological Sustainability

Inevitably, bringing a canal back to life which has lain dormant for 200 years means that some clearance of natural growth cannot be avoided. Part of the aims of restoration is to create a corridor rich in both plant and animal wildlife. As well as creating rich habitats in the water and its margins with the land, this enables wildlife to migrate safely from one area to another, increasing the ecological diversity of the area through which it passes. There need be no conflict between restoration and conservation. If a restoration scheme is well managed there need be no lasting concern when trees are felled or scrub growth removed. While there will always be short-term damage as areas are cleared and heavy equipment moves around on a site, the permanent gain

Commercial and Environmental Sustainability

which will follow far outweighs the temporary disruption which occurs and, even without human help, nature quickly recovers. With help, it recovers faster and stronger and a richer environment is the result. A number of British canals are Sites of Special Scientific Interest, providing safe homes for bats and other protected species as well as carrying regular traffic both by boat and on foot.

There are, of course, constraints. Before any restoration can begin, an independent, professional ecological survey must be commissioned to identify any issues which may affect the project. Some are legal, especially with regard to protected species, and nesting wild birds or mammals, but others are simply good practice even if not required by law. Equally important are positive measures which can be taken to encourage the diversity of wildlife along the canal.

Figure 7: Native saplings being planted at Moat Farm (Paul Henshaw)

Where the restored canal passes through woodland and trees must be removed, at least as many replacement trees are planted using appropriate native species. Usually these will be of a greater number and variety than those removed. This has been particularly important at the Kymin East and Moat Farm sites.

Where existing trees are retained most will have been un-managed for many years and a programme of active management, as advised by professional arborists, is undertaken to ensure healthy growth and the safety of users of the canal and towpath.

When trees are felled and brushwood cleared, much of the wood is closely stacked to allow it to slowly rot away to provide a home for a multitude of invertebrates which form an essential part of food chain supporting the more visible mammal and bird species. In years gone by restoration volunteers, especially during the winter, would take great delight in building huge bonfires in the countryside, but this is a far better way of dealing with this material, in Mother Nature's own way – as She has done for millions of years.

Commercial and Environmental Sustainability

Figure 8: Logs piled up to rot away to provide a rich habitat for invertebrates (Paul Henshaw)

Although a protected species, slow worms are fairly common at the Malswick site and great care was taken to disturb them as little as possible and to provide a protective reptile barrier. One of the easiest and most rewarding ways of working with nature is to provide nesting boxes especially designed to attract particular species of birds. Various types have been put up at several different sites, and in some cases, in buildings, nearby.

The mature canal corridor of water and towpath vegetation with its abundant and varied invertebrate populations also encourages bats to roost in specially designed bat boxes.

The *Woodland Trust* estimates that around 118,000 miles of hedgerows have been destroyed since 1950, due largely to intensification of agriculture and wherever possible the Trust plants hedging to further encourage wildlife.

Figure 9: 5-star bug hotel at Moat Farm (Paul Henshaw)

177

Commercial and Environmental Sustainability

Many metres of new hedges have been planted at Malswick and Llanthony. Even more will follow as other lengths of the canal are developed.

Figure 10: Slow worms at Malswick (Alan McBride)

Environmental sustainability comes at a cost in both time and money. It can be frustrating to teams of volunteers who can't wait to start work, to have to delay until it can be proven that great crested newts are totally absent from a site or that there are no active bat roosts high in the surrounding trees. An expert independent survey is expensive and time-consuming, but is but one part of the preliminary effort which always has to be undertaken before work can begin on the ground.

However, the rewards are great. A well-managed waterway can provide a far richer natural environment than the sterility of an abandoned railway line or even a grassy field. Invertebrates, fish, amphibians, reptiles, mammals, and birds, together with fungi, plants and trees can all thrive in both urban and rural canals to give pleasure to us all.

Figure 11: Owl box under construction at Moat Farm

The Canal Trust's Fleet

The Trust owns five boats, all currently moored in Over Basin – two trip boats and three "heritage boats" which were acquired from British Waterways initially on a lease basis, but with the prospect of Trust ownership.

The trip boat Mister Maysey, is named after the William Maysey who worked for the canal company for 35 years from the time of its building from Gloucester. He had various roles including assistant engineer, manager and general factotum, and had a reputation of getting things done. The boat was purchased by the Trust from the IWA West Country Branch in 1999 where she had served as the trip boat RUBY II on the Bridgwater and Taunton Canal. She was brought to Oxenhall where initial restoration work was carried out. She was then moved to Over in time for the opening of the basin in 2000.

Since then her superstructure has been almost entirely replaced, the interior refurbished and repairs to the hull undertaken. Painted in the Trust's yellow and black colours and with an eye-catching name scroll she now carries visitors along the newly restored length of the canal on Over Open Days.

Figure 1: The newly renovated Mister Maysey at the Over Canal Festival in 2012

The Trust also owns three boats which had been part of the British Waterways Heritage Fleet. Following a decision in 2005 to modernise its fleet of

The Canal Trust's Fleet

workboats, British Waterways auctioned much of its old fleet, but a number were leased to voluntary organisations who were required to restore them to a satisfactory standard, and if that was achieved by the end of the lease, the boat would then become theirs.

In 2007 the Trust acquired Alder on this basis. Alder has an interesting history. Originally built by Yarwoods in 1931, as a Bolinder-powered motor, she became Fellows, Morton and Clayton No. 301. In 1965 she was converted by British Waterways at the Bradley yard into two work boats. Alder is the stern of the original FMC narrow boat fitted with a new bow and a Lister HR2 engine. Now only 37' long, she worked as a push tug on the Kennet and Avon Canal.

She arrived at Over from Devizes on October 15th on a low-loader and was craned into the basin after maintenance and repairs to the hull and the fitting of a new propeller. Much work has been done to bring her to her present excellent condition in H&G livery and Alder is now in the Trust's ownership.

Figure 2: Alder sharing water space with boats from the Gloucester Model Boat Club in August 2013 (Ted Beagles)

The second member of the BW Heritage Fleet to be acquired is the tug Renton. Also built by Yarwoods, Renton began life in 1936 as a full-length motor in the Grand Union Canal Carriers fleet, a Large Northwich Town Class.

After work on the Grand Union between London and Birmingham she was converted by the War Department in 1943 into a 48' ice-breaker, subsequently acquiring a more conventional bow. In 2009 the Trust secured the lease and was able to bring the boat by water under her own power from Marsworth on the Grand Union Canal to Gloucester. This was a trip of 147 miles and 165 locks, undertaken by a Trust director and her family, complete with dog, in eight days, even though the tug was not fitted out with living accommodation.

The Canal Trust's Fleet

Figure 3: Renton at Over basin in September 2012 (Ted Beagles)

While in Gloucester Docks undergoing restoration, Renton was called upon to assist with several tasks on the Gloucester and Sharpness Canal including the rescue of the National Waterways Museum's large trip boat Boadicea which was drifting around in the Docks having suffered an engine failure with a party of schoolchildren aboard.

In 2011 Renton arrived by low-loader at Over and was craned into the basin, where she now acts as a trip boat on Open Days and cruises up and down the canal, her 23" propeller helping to control the weed which summer weather inevitably encourages.

The third of the Heritage Boats is the smallest, and newest. Bosley, a push tug was built in 1986 and used by British Waterways on the Trent and Mersey Canal and the River Weaver. She has a large winch at the bows and will be a useful small vessel as restoration of the canal continues. She was acquired by the Trust in 2011.

Figure 4: Bosley at Over in August 2013 (Ted Beagles)

181

The Canal Trust's Fleet

Figure 5: The heritage boats at Over in 2022 (Debbie Barber)

British Waterways was clearly content that the Trust was caring for and using the boats to its satisfaction. All three leases were terminated early and the boats sold to the Trust for one pound each. Bearing in mind that three of the Trust's boats are elderly to say the least, two being around 90 years old, they require much care and attention to keep them in good condition. Fortunately the Trust has a team of volunteers with considerable experience and expertise who are able to source or manufacture replacement parts when necessary.

A more recent acquisition is a second Trip Boat, Susan. This has an electric outboard motor which originally received its power from a steam powered generator. This has now been converted to "plug-in" battery power which now provides for an almost silent cruise along the canal.

Figure 6: Susan at Over in 2022

Following an extensive training programme, by 2022 the Trust had a team of six volunteers with Helmsman Certificates enable them to legally operate its trip boats.

The Canal in the Community

From the earliest days of the Herefordshire and Gloucestershire Canal Society it was established that any part of the canal which was restored was not just for the benefit of land owners, boaters and anglers but for the entire community. As has already been noted, most people who visit waterways do so by foot or bicycle and although they may not contribute to any of the associated costs, they enjoy the benefits it affords which the Trust wholeheartedly encourages. The use of the canal by community organisations and businesses enables the canal to be enjoyed by ever greater numbers of people and encourages local support for the overall vision of a fully navigable canal between the two cities.

Most community activity is focussed on Over Basin where there is a reasonable stretch of canal and the water-space of the basin itself. One of the first groups to use the basin was the Gloucester and District Model Boat Club which took part in the opening of the Basin in 2000. Although the Club operates at a number of locations in Gloucestershire it regards Over as 'home'.

Figure 1: A small flotilla of boats built by members of the Gloucester and District Model Boats Club.
(Ted Tedaldi)

Anyone who thinks that model boats are kids' stuff needs to visit Over to see the models on the water. Highly detailed, radio-controlled and full of electronic gadgetry these certainly aren't toys – not even 'big boys toys'. Or girls'.

The Canal in the Community

On days when the Trust's boats are also running there is a wonderful mix of craft, the highly manoueverable models ensuring there are no collisions.

Figure 2: Members of the Club with their boats on a chilly day at Over Basin (Ted Tedaldi)

In the very hot summer of 2022 fourteen Club members, including three ladies, removed about 80 barrowsful of weed from the basin which not only helped the modellers but everyone else who uses the Basin - including the Canal Trust.

Another group which began using the Basin very early on was Sailing4Disabled which helps people of mixed abilities to get onto the water. Now operating as Rowing Pirates the group has two Katakanus, each taking up to six people. A Katakanu, as its name suggests, is like two canoes fixed together to form an extraordinarily stable but manoeuvrable catamaran. The group also has an electrically powered Wheelyboat, a totally wheelchair-accessible boat enabling anyone to enjoy a trip along the canal without having to power it themselves!

The group also has an itBikes Water Bike which allows the rider to pedal their way along the canal. Like the Katakanu, this is a totally stable craft which enables less-able people to enjoy the canal in complete safety.

It is unlikely that the early founders of the Herefordshire and Gloucestershire Canal Society, would ever have imagined that such craft as these would ever travel down "their" canal, but they believed the canal was for everyone and we are now seeing something of that dream coming true. In these days of 'inclusivity' the Canal Trust tries to enable everyone to enjoy being on the water. It is justly proud of this and hopes to extend this to Hereford when the Aylestone Basin is built. Stephen Ballard would be delighted!

The Canal in the Community

Figure 3: Happy young people in a KataKanu in 2022 (Pete Bisson)

Figure 4: An itBikes Waterbike in action at Over in 2014 (Pete Bisson)

It is especially gratifying when young people become involved with the canal as this can sometimes lead to a lifetime interest pleasure in our waterways. In June 2022 Scouts from South Herefordshire came to help cut back some of the undergrowth at Kymin and returned the following week to help prepare the towpath for the Herefordshire Walking Festival the following weekend.

The Canal in the Community

In September 2021 scouts from the 1st Cheltenham Scout Group came to Over basin bringing with them their boats made from nothing more than cardboard and sticky tape. Some were more successful than others and not everyone remained dry but by all accounts a thoroughly good time was had by all.

Figures 5, 6 & 7: Scouts in their magnificently sturdy cardboard craft propelled by cardboard paddles, ready to head off to Hereford (Jeremy Gibbs)

Whether this proves that getting onto the water need not be as expensive as many believe might be a moot point, but it certainly proves that it is possible for boys and girls to have a great time in the open air without their smartphones.

Not all the groups who visit the canal are water based and some surprising visitors have been working on the canal with the Trust. In 2018 a group of ten members of the Audit Team of Wells Fargo Bank UK came to Oxenhall and Malswick for a two day "volunteer experience".

An experience it certainly was - at Malswick they helped with clearing the line of the canal through the east woodland and spent some time splitting and bagging logs which will be sold to raise funds for the Trust.

At Oxenhall they attacked the ever-present encroachment of reeds and weeds, of which there were plenty. Wet vegetation is very heavy and getting it out of the canal is extremely hard work, very different from the day-to-day routine of the Bank.

It was intended to be an enjoyable experience in the fresh air of the Gloucestershire countryside and there was plenty to show for it at the end of the two days. The members of the groups were rotated between the sites to provide a variety of aches and pains.

The Canal in the Community

Figure 8: Auditors from Wells Fargo UK hard at work at Oxenhall (Brian Fox)

Other Reminders

While the Trust has been working hard to restore navigation along the canal, others have been quietly preserving some of the remaining buildings and other features which were to be seen along the towpath in years gone by. These are not museum pieces – they are privately owned homes which form part of the vernacular architecture of the two counties.

Some are now quite isolated, being built where they were needed to perform a particular function. The only significant cluster of buildings is to be found close to the site of the wharf at Withington Marsh. The house of William Bird, the Wharfinger, has been sensitively restored in recent years and within a few yards of this is a terrace of houses which may well have been lengthsmens' cottages.

Figure 1: The signage on William Bird's wharf cottage at Withington, now barely visible.

Figure 2: Lengthsmens' Cottages at Withington Wharf (Author)

188

Other Reminders

Another house which stood at the end of an arm at the wharf bore the word SALT on its end wall, almost invisible today, but indicating its origin as a salt warehouse.

Figure 3: The Salt Warehouse at Withington Wharf (Author)

One of the largest buildings dating from the operational period of the canal is a short distance away from the wharf at Withington Marsh in Wyatt Lane, standing by the canal bridge which is now scarcely visible.

It is believed that the house was built about the time the canal opened to Hereford to accommodate the "superintendent". Unlike most of other surviving buildings which were brick-built, this was constructed mainly of stone but, like several others features an unusual asymmetrical roof, similar to a "saltbox roof", with the longest slope to the rear of the building.

Figure 4: 'Little Lugg', formerly the "superintendent's" house. (Author)

Other Reminders

While the building has been greatly modernised, many original features remain. It is clear that the part of house nearest the canal was used for storage, or perhaps as a warehouse. The cobbled floor still survives and high up on the wall, at the level of the first story there is evidence of a door which has since been bricked up.

Almost certainly there would have been a hoist above it to haul materials into the building from a wharf adjacent to the bridge. When traffic along this section of the canal ceased around 1885 the house was then used as pub – *The Bridge Inn*.

In 1962 the building was considerably modernised and was bought by the present owners in 1965. One of the Trust's committees meets regularly in the spacious and elegant dining room.

Only two of the original lock keeper's cottages have survived, both being Grade II listed in 1985. The stone-built lock cottage at Withington, where the lock is buried in the garden, is in excellent condition but has been much modified over the years.

Figure 5: Lock cottage at Withington (By kind permission of the owner)

A mile away towards Gloucester at Kymin is *Canal House*, almost certainly another wharfinger's house, again featuring an asymmetrical roof but constructed entirely of brick. The wharfinger may well have also acted as the lock keeper at Kymin Lock a few hundred yards along the towpath. It is now an attractive home.

Other Reminders

Figure 6: Canal House at Kymin (Author)

While there were three tunnels on the canal only one tunnel keeper's cottage survives today. The tunnel keeper's cottage at Ashperton, was quickly built in 1842 by Stephen Ballard so that he could live on the site and supervise the work of excavating the very deep cuttings on either side of the tunnel.

The cottage was almost derelict before being beautifully restored. It stands high above the canal portal at the top of the deep cutting and carries a plaque reminding passers-by of its function, the tunnel itself being out of sight from the road.

Figure 7: The near -derelict Tunnel Cottage at Ashperton (Mike Potts)

Figure 8: The restored Tunnel Cottage standing high above the canal at Ashperton (Neil Smith)

Figure 9: A tile made by Robert Ballard in his Ledbury works found in the garden of Tunnel Cottage (Neil Smith)

Figure 10: The cosy interior of Tunnel Cottage (Neil Smith)

Further along the canal towards Ledbury a pair of canal cottages stand on Swinmoor Common, with no road access. These were almost certainly lengthsmens' cottages as there was no wharf or lock nearby.

Other Reminders

Figure 11: The lengthmens' cottages at Swinmoor (Nigel Jefferies)

A much finer building, also once derelict, is the wharf house at Staplow, one of Stephen Ballard's most elegant houses.

Figure 12: The Wharf House at Staplow (Nigel Jefferies)

Although the railway line had avoided Oxenhall, some of the property associated with the canal eventually passed to British Railways which sold it

Other Reminders

during the 1960s including the lock cottage at House Lock, the building having survived a lightning strike in 1956. It was built by Stephen Ballard in 1838 and, for a lock cottage, it is extremely elegant in its design with a number of interesting architectural features. It is, however, essentially a "two up and two down". At the time of the 1851 census housed the lock keeper, Richard Goode, his wife Eliza, their five children and two lodgers who were colliers!

Over time the property had deteriorated to the point where Newent District Council issued a Demolition Order on the semi-derelict property, probably because the tenant's wife had recently had a baby and this was the surest way of getting the family to the top of the waiting list for council housing. There was no electricity to the property, the only water supply being a polluted well and the only sanitation an outside privy.

Figure 13: The derelict House Lock cottage in the 1960's (Mike Potts)

Unaware that they were selling the property to one of their employees, which, had they known, would have complicated matters greatly, British Railways finally completed the sale to Robin Stiles in 1967.

The new owner carried out an agreed Schedule of Works including repairs to the roof and installation of a water supply and septic tank drainage. The Demolition Order was revoked in 1969, the building being Grade II listed in 1985 and is now a delightful home.

Other Reminders

Figure 14: The restored House Lock in 2004 (Author)

The Road Ahead

It would be a brave and perhaps foolish person who would commit a view of the future of any canal restoration to print. Hopes are raised and dashed in equal measure and success in one area is often accompanied by delays in another. About the only forecast one can make with any confidence is that it will take much longer than one would ever imagine. If we are like Jane Austen's Mrs. Dashwood and Marianne, for whom "to wish was to hope, and to hope was to expect" we will almost certainly be disappointed.

But, because many readers will be as much interested in the future as the past, something must be said about our Road Ahead. For the working boatmen of the past, the "road ahead" meant the state of the canal towards their destination and a clear road ahead is what they always dreamed of. Our road ahead is far from clear but experience elsewhere has shown us that, while canal restoration is invariably a long and challenging process, nothing should be written off as impossible – a lesson learned from the restoration of the Huddersfield Narrow Canal. Once dubbed the "impossible restoration", it fully re-opened to traffic in 2001.

While, in strictly engineering terms, the Hereford and Gloucester Canal is not an easy restoration, there is nothing to be done that has not been achieved elsewhere. Between Hereford and Ledbury parts of the canal have remained in water for nearly 200 years, most of the bridges still stand, the two tunnels are believed to be in relatively good condition and only three locks need to be rebuilt. One new main road bridge, on the Roman Road, has already been provided as well as those at Farriers Way in Hereford.

The greatest engineering challenge in Herefordshire will be to design a new aqueduct over the Lugg which must pass over the river without impedance of its flow, especially when in flood. For the River Lugg there are no general requirements as to the height above river level required, each crossing being considered individually by the Environment Agency, but it is almost certain that the historic level will not be sufficiently high above the river. While the river must be crossed if the canal is to reach Hereford, there are possible alternatives to the low aqueduct built by Stephen Ballard in 1884.

A mile or so away the canal passed under the Hereford-Worcester railway line and although some of the masonry of the original culvert under the railway embankment at Shelwick may still exist, the best solution may be to take the canal off-line and thrust-bore a new culvert. The embankment is high and thrust-boring beneath it would not constitute a particularly difficult feat of engineering. The major issues will be the cost and obtaining the agreement of Network Rail.

Figure 1: The railway embankment at Shelwick. The canal passed under the embankment some yards to the left of the road.

New main road bridges under the A4103 at Monkhide, the A465 at Withington, the A438 at Ledbury and the A417 at Canon Frome will be required. However, these main roads are unlike main roads in other parts of the Midlands where Herefordshire main roads are often considered to be little more than country lanes. All of these bridges can be rebuilt without significant changes of road level.

The canal line through Ledbury, with its five deep locks, is too obstructed to afford a practical route for restoration, but the River Leadon corridor, which bypasses the town to the west through the Riverside Park offers a pleasant alternative route which is protected in the Local Development Plan. More and shallower locks will probably be built to better fit in with the landscape and assist in water management.

Between Ledbury and Gloucester, restoration will be far more difficult. Much less of the canal is in water, most of the line having been infilled for the railway. Of the 22 original locks, 14 are on this section including the deep river lock at Over.

The Road Ahead

The old canal crossed the B4215 no less than four times and the original bridges are long gone, but here the re-positioning of some locks and the rebuilding of the canal at a different level offer possible solutions.

This section also includes the mile and a quarter long Oxenhall Tunnel which caused so much grief to the original builders of the canal. A major threat to restoration was the planned route of a high-pressure gas pipeline of four feet diameter. The construction of this, crossing just above the tunnel and with the subsequent restricted zone around it, would have prevented work on the tunnel and its eventual use for navigation.

Negotiations with Transco's project manager took place at The Wharf House, with views of Over Basin and maps of the canal on the wall, and led eventually to an agreement in 2008 that the pipeline specification would be modified, at a cost of some £300,000, to allow the Trust unrestricted access to the tunnel for both restoration and navigation.

The masonry at the southern end is thought to be in remarkably good condition and this gives way to a long section which is unlined and formed by the natural rock. The last part at the northern end of the tunnel has partially or totally collapsed and the northern portal has almost completely disappeared. The restoration of Oxenhall Tunnel will be eye-wateringly expensive but most large and successful canal restorations have had a similar project to contend with and have found ways to achieve success.

Near Newent wharf, to the north of the town the old canal passed beneath the B4215 Newent-Dymock road at Lambs Barn Pitch near the Newent Fire Station. Here the railway, having avoided Oxenhall Tunnel, diverged from the canal line and was carried over the road by a short viaduct. The road was lowered to achieve this and it is said that the canal at its original level now cannot pass under it.

A simple solution to this, used on many canals, would be to use a swing or lift bridge to carry the road over the canal. Traffic lights, controlled by the boat crews, would stop road traffic while the boats pass through. Some of these bridges elsewhere on the network cross busier roads than B4215 at Newent but it is highly unlikely that any such arrangement for a new crossing would be entertained today.

For many years the proposed solution was to use the abutments of the viaduct, suitably heightened to conform to modern road building standards, to carry an aqueduct over the road. The required height, however is considerably above that of the canal on either side. On the Oxenhall side it was proposed

The Road Ahead

to omit the bottom two locks of the Oxenhall flight and carry the canal over the Ell Brook and the former Willows Nursery site on a long embankment and build staircase locks on the Malswick side of the aqueduct to take the canal down to its original level.

Figure 2: The railway viaduct abutments at Lambs Barn Pitch (Illia Kobziev)

The embankment through the Willows Nursery site would have had to be up to 20' high in places. Given the known and understandable objections from the owners of nearby properties and the likely difficulty in gaining planning permission, proposals are now being considered to carry boats from the canal on an inclined plane up to the level of the old Newent station and then over the road with another inclined plane on the other side to take them down again.

Boats would be hauled out of the water on a wheeled cradle running on rails along the planes, through a restored Newent Station and over the road. Though never in common use, inclined planes were once a feature of some British canals but only the one at Blists Hill museum survives today.

There are several modern inclined planes in continental Europe, some built on a vast scale and carrying large boats or ships. The only operational inclined plane in Britain would undoubtedly be an important visitor attraction for the area.

There may be a further possibility, less exciting but simpler, which I have never heard suggested by the Trust. This would mostly retain the original level of the canal though the former Willows site but it would pass under the

The Road Ahead

B4215 road by means of a drop lock. Historically, these have not been regarded as good practice on the grounds of safety and excessive water use but the sophisticated broad drop lock at Dalmuir on the Forth and Clyde Canal has been in constant use without incident since 2002.

Figure 3: A boat beginning its journey up the inclined plane on the Elblag Canal in Poland
(Wikimedia)

An even simpler and completely safe arrangement without the need for complex safety mechanisms could be adopted at Newent, using a lock either side of the road with a short pound below it, pumping the water from one lock to the other through a side pond when necessary. I am not in a position to determine how much the road has been lowered and therefore the depth of such locks required but it would be surprising if it was very great.

In fact, the Ell Brook, which runs at much the same level as the canal once did at this point, passes easily under the B4215 only a few yards away from the site of the old railway viaduct. Perhaps the received wisdom that the road has been lowered so much as to make it impossible for the canal to pass under it might not be quite so cut and dried after all. A simple road bridge, perhaps slightly raised above the present road level would not, of course, be a great visitor attraction!

The river lock at Over is historically something of a mystery. The original scheme for the canal planned to join the Severn at some point in the Eastern Channel then crossing Alney Island and the West Channel by an aqueduct.

The Road Ahead

It appears that this scheme was abandoned and Over Lock built to drop the canal into the Western Channel.

Looking at it today from Over Basin it is difficult to estimate how deep the lock would need to be, especially as it depends upon the state of the tide. Some have estimated it to be as much as 30' deep, by far the deepest narrow lock ever built in Britain but it is difficult to believe that a 30' lock at Over was built and used without any contemporary comment. There were accidents at Over but these seem to have involved boats leaving the lock and joining the river rather than any difficulty with the lock itself.

Given that access from the river may have to be limited to certain times either side of high tide there are arguments for rebuilding the lock as a broad one, taking two boats at a time, which would also help to make access easier. Against this is the fact that a deep, broad lock requires twice as much water as a narrow one.

In 2021 members of the Trust met informally with an Honorary Consulting Engineer from the Inland Waterways Association to consider what other options there might be for linking the canal to the river

Some require the rebuilding of Over Lock and others an aqueduct over the Severn from Over Basin and a cut across Alney Island with a lock dropping the canal into the Eastern Channel. There are pros and cons for all the options and these were outlined in *The Wharfinger* Edition 154 and comments were invited from Trust members. This marks a welcome change of policy, as in the past the Trust Board has seemed reluctant to share their thoughts on issues such as these. Formerly, when the board has undertaken or commissioned options reports, these have never been made public, even in summary form.

Finally, we must return to Hereford where more than 20 years ago an area close to the city centre was identified as the site of the terminal basin around which shops, restaurants and hotels would be built rather in the fashion of Brindley Place in Birmingham. Unfortunately, and some would say, unbelievably, the new Link Road opened in 2017 cuts off the site reserved for the basin from the rest of the canal.

Discussions with the City Council have begun to identify a possible alternative site on the other side of the Link Road near the railway station. Progress has been made, but it is unlikely that it can be as spacious and offer the commercial and leisure opportunities as the original plans had provided for.

The Road Ahead

But as one opportunity closes another may open. Adjacent to the canal in Aylestone Park is an area of the park which is frequently waterlogged and unusable for sporting purposes. This may present the opportunity to develop an additional basin, a community basin, on the outskirts of the City, but still only a mile and a half from High Town. This could be specifically designed to provide the sort of facilities enjoyed by community groups at Over Basin opening a broader concept to the existing use of the park.

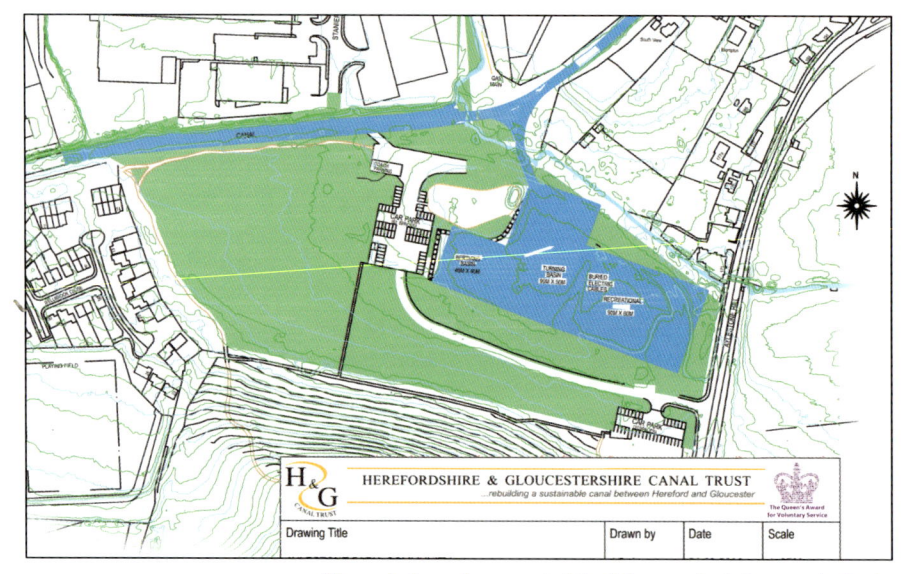

Figure 4: An early concept of the Aylestone Park Community Basin

By far the greatest challenge is not one of engineering at all, it is of land ownership. Following the closure of the canal, the land in Herefordshire was sold, or even given away. On the nationalisation of the railways in 1948 the Ledbury-Gloucester line passed into the ownership of British Railways and this land was sold off piecemeal after the railway closed in 1964.

Over both counties, possession of the line of the canal is now shared by over 100 landowners, some sympathetic towards restoration, some indifferent and a few who oppose it. The Trust has acquired or now has legal access to some short lengths, but one of the major priorities over the coming years must be to build up its land holding wherever it can.

This may be achieved by outright purchase, if the necessary capital is available, and the Trust has a Land Fund for this purpose. Land may also be obtained under agreements with developers or others where a mutual benefit will be secured. The Malswick section of the canal and the canal and basin at Over were acquired by this means.

It will be a long time before boats from Gloucester arrive in Hereford again, but when they do, it will be because of the hundreds of people who worked tirelessly over those many years to make it happen.

As I wrote in my introduction, it does not matter whether they have been out in all weathers getting muddy, at a desk preparing paperwork, representing the Trust in negotiations or promoting the Trust at a show – all will have played a vital role in bringing this beautiful canal back to life.

Writing in 1979, David Bick was right in observing that:

"*Throughout the length and breadth of England, no major navigation is so lost in obscurity as the Hereford and Gloucester Canal.*"

That certainly cannot be said today!

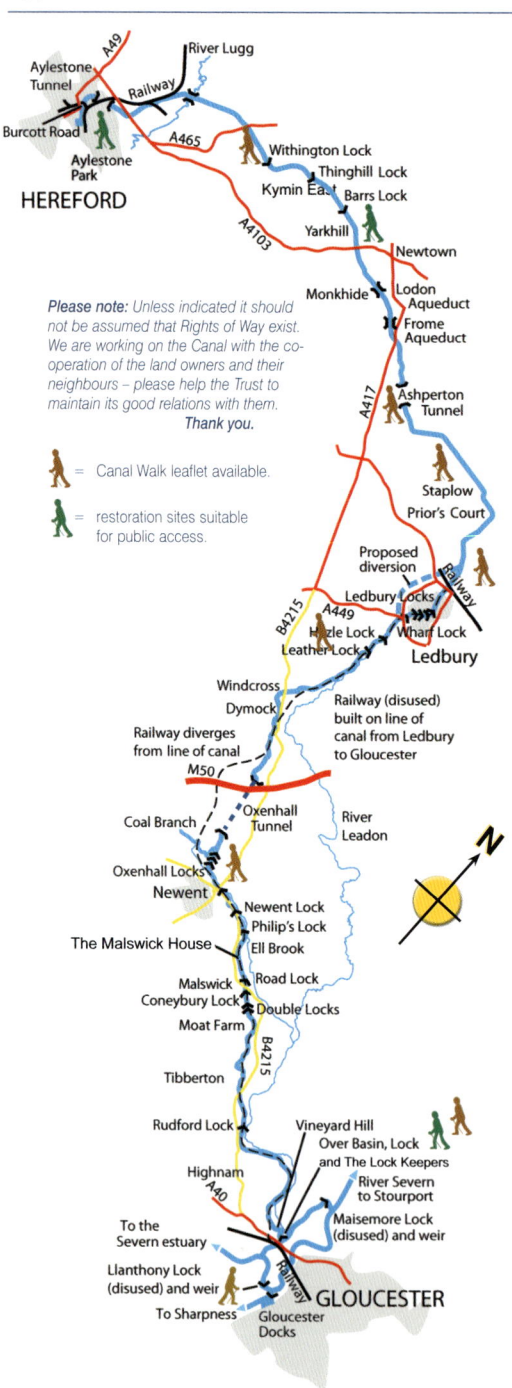

Appendix

Mileage Table:

Mileage from Over	Feature
3½	Rudford Lock
3¾	Rudford Bridge
6	Double Locks
6¼	Coneybury Lock
6½	Road Lock
7½	Philip's Lock
8	Newent Lock
8¾	Newent Wharf
9	Devin's Lock or Oxenhall Bottom Lock
9¼	Oxenhall Top Lock
9¾	Oxenhall Tunnel South Portal
11	Oxenhall Tunnel North Portal
11½	Boyce Court
12	Dymock
15	Leather Lock
15¾	Hazle Lock
16¼	Old Wharf, Ledbury
17	New Wharf, Ledbury
19½	Priors Court
20	Staplow Wharf
22½	Ashperton Tunnel East Portal
22¾	Ashperton Tunnel West Portal
24	Canon Frome Wharf
26	Crews Pitch, Monkhide
26¾	Barr's Lock
27¾	Kymin Lock
28¾	Withington Lock
29½	Withington Marsh Wharf
31	Lugg Aqueduct
31¾	Shelwick Green
32¾	Aylestone Tunnel East Portal
33	Aylestone Tunnel West Portal
34	Hereford, Barr's Court Basin

Please note: Unless indicated it should not be assumed that Rights of Way exist. We are working on the Canal with the co-operation of the land owners and their neighbours – please help the Trust to maintain its good relations with them. Thank you.

= Canal Walk leaflet available.

= restoration sites suitable for public access.

Map based on original by Martin Ludgate, Canal Boat Magazine.

204

Appendix

Boats moored on the Canal on April 7th 1861

Compiled by John Chappell from 1861 Census dataThe four boats named The

Boat Name	Tonnage	Home Wharf	Location on April 7th
Colina	30	Gloucester	
Lion	30		
Mary	30	Gloucester	
Mary Ann	28		
Perseverance	28		
Perseverance	30		
Ralph	30		
	30		Canon Frome Wharf
Lady of the Lake*	27		Dymock
Unknown			
Thomas			
Useful			
Betsy			
Sand Bank			
Ellen	20		
William	22		
Perseverance			
Perseverance No. 3			

*Details of Lady of the Lake are as of 1871

The four boats named Perseverance were owned by members of the Whitehouse family who seem to have used this as a fleet name. Presumably they were numbered, but this were not always recorded by the enumerator. They were associated with the canal for the whole of its operational life.

In the census of 1871 the distribution of boats was as follows:

Hereford	0
Gloucester	1
Newent	4
Oxenhall	1

Appendix

People from Newent recorded as involved with boats in 1861

Compiled by John Chappell from 1861 Census data

Address	Name	Age	Dependants	Job	Notes
New Street	Charles Jones	35	4	Boatman	
	Pamphrey	23	2	Boatman	
	Charles Mayo	14	0	Boatman	
	John Mayo	21	0	Boatman	
	Charles Wood	19		Boatman	
Rocks Ally	Whitehouse	23	0	Boatman	
Rocks Ally	Charles Pitt	16		Boatman	
Church Street	William Chandler	26	3	Boatman	
Church Street	George Williams	21	0	Boatman	
Broad Street Police Station	Francis Cousier	24	0	Boatman	In custody
Lower New Street	Charles Thomas	49	0	Boatman	
Lower New Street	James Jones	71	1	Boatman	
Lower New Street	Edward Thomas	21	0	Boatman	Edward and Henry are brothers
Lower New Street	Henry Thomas	19	0	Boatman	
Lower New Street	Henry Jones	29	4	Boatman	
New Street	William Hatch	45	2	Grocer and Boat Owner	
New Street	Fredrick Hatch	20	0	Boatman	William's Nephew
Hill Top (Near Stardens)	William Jones	26	0	Boatman	

Gypsy Queen demonstrates at Over Festival how canal boats were towed years ago. *(Ted Beagles)*

Index

A

Alney Island   16, 20, 62, 200, 209

Aqueduct   9, 16, 20, 39, 78–80, 133, 136–138, 196, 198–201, 204, 209

Ashperton   9, 17, 33, 47, 65, 78, 108, 191–192, 210

Aylestone   121–128, 184, 202

Aylestone Tunnel   38, 74, 78, 127–128

B

Philip Ballard   38, 47, 49, 61, 75, 77

Stephen Ballard   24–25, 28, 31, 34, 37–40, 41–43, 45, 49–50, 75, 77, 86, 88, 91, 95, 114, 116, 171, 184, 191, 193–194, 196, 209–210

Barrs Lock   116–119

David Bick   1–2, 92, 99–100, 203

John Biddulph   24–25, 43

Boyce Court   81, 84, 209

Thomas Brassey   44

James Brindley   7, 8

British Waterways   89, 104–105, 107, 149, 165, 168–169, 170, 179–182

Bromyard   7, 30

C

Canal and River Trust   i–ii, 64, 104, 110, 168, 170

Canal Festival   107, 109, 149, 179

Canon Frome   25, 34–35, 44, 56, 86, 90, 197, 204–205

John Carne   16

Josiah Clowes   8–9, 13–14, 16–18, 33

D

Dymock   14, 17, 53, 57, 62, 65, 70–72, 75, 81, 84, 108, 209

E

Eastnor Castle   iii, 23, 108

Ell Brook Aqueduct   133, 137–138, 209

F

Forest of Dean   iii, 4, 7, 12, 23, 56, 103, 133, 139

River Frome   9, 21, 23, 79

Frome Aqueduct   78–80

G

Gloucester   2, 4–5, 7, 8, 10, 13–15, 16, 19–20, 27–30, 38, 40, 46, 52–57, 59, 61–62, 65, 78, 81, 88, 90, 100, 106, 109, 111, 130, 134, 140, 150, 154, 161, 168, 173–174, 179–181, 183, 190, 197, 202–203, 209, 211

Gloucester and District Model Boat Club   1 0 7 , 109

Great Western   52, 56–57, 65–66

H

Charles Hadfield   i, 99–100

Richard Hall   8

Hugh Henshall   13–14

Hereford   4, i, 2, 4–7, 8–15, 21–23, 25–30, 32, 34, 36–37, 39–40, 41, 44–45, 47, 49, 51–56, 59–61, 63, 65–66, 67, 69, 71, 74–77, 78, 80, 89, 92, 95, 97, 99–101, 106, 113–114, 116, 120–122, 124–126, 128, 147, 184, 189, 196, 201, 203, 209, 211–212

207

Index

Hereford and Gloucester Canal 3, i, 1–2, 15, 20, 24, 34–35, 39, 43–44, 53–54, 57, 60–61, 68, 70, 74–75, 88–90, 113, 165, 196, 203, 212

Herefordshire 7, 20, 29, 37–38, 40, 52, 65, 77, 84, 102–103, 108, 111, 112, 121, 127, 135, 168, 185, 196–197, 202, 209–210

Herefordshire and Gloucestershire Canal Society 80, 92

Heritage Boats 4, 107, 109, 179, 181–182

Hodgetts 71

Joseph Holloway 53, 68–69, 71, 75–76

House Lock 88, 100–101, 130, 133–136, 194–195, 209

I

Inland Waterways Association 97, 99, 107, 201

K

Kymin 2, 88, 119–121, 176, 185, 190–191, 204

L

Leadon 8, 44, 141, 145, 149, 197, 210

Ledbury ii, iii, 8, 10–13, 16–17, 19–28, 30–31, 32–33, 35–37, 44–47, 52–57, 59–61, 64–66, 68–69, 73–76, 78, 81, 84, 86–88, 108, 130, 134, 192, 196–197, 202

Leominster Canal 7, 8, 20, 28–30

Llanthony 89, 165, 168

Llanthony Hydro 168–169

Llanthony Lock 108, 165–169

River Lugg 8–9, 28–29, 39, 79, 196

Lugg Aqueduct 78–79, 204

M

Maisemore 89, 99, 165, 168, 209

Malswick 23, 150, 154–157, 161–163, 177–178, 186, 199, 203

Malswick House 161, 175

William Maysey 17, 23–25, 179

Mister Maysey 107, 145–146, 150, 179

Moat Farm 150–155, 176–178

Monkhide 24, 95, 98, 108, 112, 114–116, 121, 197, 204

Monkhide Skew Bridge 4, 35, 116

N

Newent 2, 8, 10, 12–14, 17–19, 21, 23, 46, 53–57, 63, 70, 72, 75, 81, 84, 86, 92, 100, 105, 138–140, 174, 194, 198–200

O

Over 15, 17–18, 20, 24, 27, 36, 56, 58, 62, 88, 101, 107–111, 135, 140–141, 143–145, 147, 149, 165, 170–171, 173, 179–182, 183–184, 186, 197–198, 200–203

Over Isolation Hospital 135, 140–141, 143, 147, 170–171

Oxenhall 4, 13, 18–19, 21, 33, 61, 65, 70, 72, 75–76, 87–90, 100–101, 108, 130–132, 135–136, 138, 155, 170, 179, 186–187, 198–199

Oxenhall Tunnel iii, 17–18, 53, 55, 57, 63, 71, 81–82, 115, 130, 132, 193, 198

P

William Philip Price 56

Priors Court 28, 90

R

Rudford 15, 16, 56, 89

S

Section 106 104, 128, 141

River Severn 4, 7, 8, 10–11, 16, 19–20, 22, 29, 35, 54, 61, 65, 89, 99, 101, 111, 140, 165, 167–169, 174, 200–201

Shelwick 196–197

Staplow 61, 90, 108, 193

Robert Stephenson 25, 43

Robin Stiles i, 87, 100, 133, 194

Sustainability 1, 37, 104–105, 111, 168, 170, 173, 175, 178

W

Ralph Walker 24, 28

Walsopthorne 34

Waterway Recovery Group (WRG) 107, 117, 119, 121–122, 143, 145, 149, 162, 166

The Wharf House 20, 85, 147, 170–174, 193, 198, 209

Wharfinger 23, 85, 188, 190

Wharfinger Magazine 1–2, 95, 102, 106, 110, 201, 212

Robert Whitworth 8, 18, 20

Worcester 4–5, 15, 35, 44, 47, 50, 52, 95, 99, 103, 113–114, 120–121, 196

Y

Yarkhill 108, 116–120, 212

208

Canal Walks

The Canal Trust has produced a series of walk leaflets which explore various parts of the Hereford & Gloucester Canal.

Canal Walk No. 1 Staplow
A circular walk along part of the former Canal at Staplow, near Ledbury, Herefordshire, which includes a number of former canal buildings. The walk is largely across grassland and field boundaries. You will have to cross some stiles and uneven ground.

Canal Walk No. 2 Withington Wharf
This circular walk follows part of the alignment of the canal and views Withington Wharf, where Stephen Ballard, who built the canal between Ledbury and Hereford and aspired to be an architect, constructed several buildings which remain in near original condition.

Canal Walk No. 3 Dymock
This walk starts at the village of Dymock, Gloucestershire, which is about four miles north of Newent, on the B4215. It takes in part of the doffodil way and the deep canal cutting at Boyce Court, and up to the former entrance to the north portal of Oxenhall Tunnel.

Canal Walk No. 4 Llanthony Lock
A circular walk from Over Basin across Alney Island nature reserve to Llanthony Lock, showing the remains of a large river lock and the lock cottages. The walk continues on to Gloucester Docks before returning to The Wharf House at Over.

Canal Walk No. 5 Oxenhall
This walk starts at Oxenhall, near Newent, Gloucestershire, on the B4215. It explores a stretch of the canal approaching the southern portal of Oxenhall Tunnel including Ell Brook Aqueduct, House Lock and Lock Cottage, built by Stephen Ballard. It also crosses the line of the former Gloucester to Ledbury Railway, built by the GWR after the closure of the canal, and views the remains of the Newent coalfield.

Canal Walk No. 6 Over
Three picturesque routes by foot or bicycle to Over Basin and The Lock Keepers (formerly The Wharf House) from Highnam, Maisemore and Gloucester Docks.

Canal Walks

Canal Walk No. 7 Ashperton
This walk starts at Ashperton Church and runs alongside the remains of the canal including a section still in water. It passes the house where the canal's engineer Stephen Ballard once lived and into beautiful countryside before returning to the canal.

Canal Walk No. 8 Ledbury
This walk starts at the Leadon Vale car park near the Ledbury bypass (Leadon Way). It incorporates the route of the canal through the town then turns back into the town, then taking a section of the Herefordshire Trail back towards the River Leadon where the canal may be re-routed around Ledbury to join its original route at the Old Wharf. It is a dog friendly walk with only a short run of wooden steps towards the end of the walk to navigate. There are no stiles. The walk can be muddy in places.

Further walks in this series are planned for the future.

The leaflets are available individually from our sales stands at Festivals and Open Days on selected dates during the summer months, or as a full set from the Shop Page on our website at **www.h-g-canal.org.uk/shop.**

All proceeds from the walk leaflets go towards the promotion and restoration of the Hereford & Gloucester Canal.

Get involved …

You might like to consider making a gift to the H&G CT during your lifetime? Alternatively, remembering the H&G CT in your Will would be a lasting legacy helping towards the restoration of the H&G Canal into a 34 mile working waterway? This will be enjoyed for leisure activities by current and future generations of visitors and in the local communities through which it passes, bringing economic and employment benefits to these areas and to the two counties.

Land Fund
The Land Fund will provide the means to negotiate the crucial new sites along the line of the Hereford & Gloucester Canal where there is no new development present or where we cannot acquire the line of the Canal by other opportunities. It is a vital fund to help us eventually restore the full length from Gloucester to Hereford.

Gift Aid
This can benefit the charity further through an income tax rebate, providing you are a relevant tax payer and meet the simple rules of Gift Aid. Additionally, if you are a higher rate tax payer, you will be eligible to reclaim tax at the higher rate. Such lifetime gifts to a charity do not count as part of your estate should you be unfortunate enough to die within seven years of making the gift, unlike gifts to individuals or non-charitable bodies. Alternatively, you might like to consider donating to the H&G CT a monthly sum paid by standing order.

Bequests
Remembering the H&G CT in your Will would be a lasting legacy helping towards the restoration of the H&G Canal. As the H&G CT is a registered charity, your legacy is subtracted from the value of your estate for tax purposes. This reduces the amount of your estate that is chargeable to inheritance tax as well as benefiting the work of the H&G CT.

The H&G CT is most grateful to everyone who has made and is considering a donation, large or small, towards the restoration of the H&G Canal.

For more details please pick up a leaflet at one of our stands or find out more on our website: **www.h-g-canal.org.uk**

Get Involved ...

Please help us to restore this beautiful waterway by joining the ...

HEREFORDSHIRE & GLOUCESTERSHIRE CANAL TRUST

Now you have read our story about the history and restoration of the Hereford and Gloucester Canal, we hope it has inspired you to help us rebuild it in its entirety.

As an independent Charity, the Herefordshire & Gloucestershire Canal Trust is reliant on public support and community involvement in the Canal restoration. This is a key to unlocking grants and sponsorship.

Become a member of the Trust - armchair members are just as welcome as muddy ones, and you may be surprised at the number of ways in which you might be able to help us.

UK annual membership rates start from as little as £15.00, whilst Life Membership starts at £300.00. You can join on-line at on website **www.h-g-canal.org.uk.** Members of the Trust receive our acclaimed quarterly magazine, The Wharfinger.

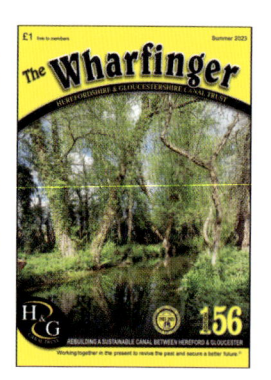

Get more involved by becoming a Trust Volunteer!

Building, brick laying, masonry, paving	Project planning and detailing
Engineering and surveying	Project development and development
Ground works, tree planting, gardening	Design, marketing and promotion
Towpath habitat creation and management	Legal work, accounting and office support
Gardening, path laying and recycling	Fundraising and grant applications
Operating plant - tractors, dumpers, excavators	Property management
Boat maintenance	Work from home

Our site teams typically each meet one day a week, and at several locations including at Oxenhall, Newent, Malswick, Over, Yarkhill, and in or around Hereford.

The office teams meet as and when needed, and generally work from home.

Please get in touch - you would be made very welcome!

www.h-g-canal.org.uk